Thank you.

To all the people who have supported me through this incredibly long and arduous process – you know who you are – and to all the people whose lives and beliefs I drew from to create this world.

To everyone who has ever offered me a ray of beauty or light or friendship in this world.

To everyone at Mount Paran North Church of God who displayed the endless grace and love of Christ to me, over and over again.

To all of my uplifting, loyal friends who have willingly been both my sounding board and my inspiration over the years.

To Lassiter High School, for the incredible opportunities and top-notch instructors and all of the laughter over the years.

To Grandma Dodie, endlessly proud of me and my accomplishments and always encouraging me.

To my wonderful family, my graceful and hilarious parents who have been the pillars of my faith all these years, and to my loving and intelligent sister who is at the same time my best friend.

Thank you all. This is for you.

To my favorite

Nathan!

Kelsie Stone

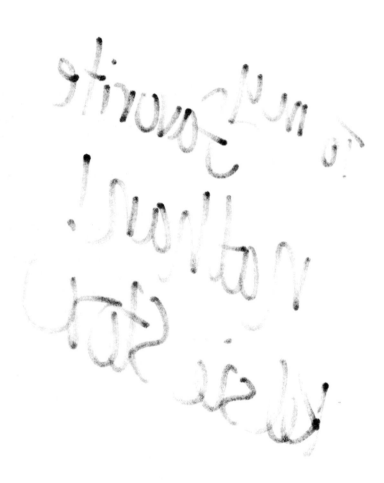

CHAPTER ONE

"Mama," I called, trailing after her. "Mama, come back."
She turned back to me and reached out, as if to touch my face.
But her hand was dripping fire, and then the fire was dust, hot,
dry dust. It trickled down my throat and I coughed, but all I
breathed was soil.

I wrenched myself upright, tangled in clammy sheets,
pulse pounding in my veins. I gulped in cool, fresh air and
looked out the window. It was just before dawn. I clambered
out of my thin bed and stood, on pale white toothpicks of legs,
gazing out at the fading stars and remembering the night we
lost Mama. Now it was just Papa and me, and Lily. Me,
Alexandria, with my dusty blonde hair, all curled and tangled.
Me, Alex, with my pale face, and my twiggy legs and arms, and
my big, brown eyes. Papa used to say that my hair was the same
color as the wheat, and that meant we were supposed to be
here. Then Mama went away and he didn't say that anymore.

Actually, Papa didn't talk much at all right after Mama
left, save telling me and Lily what to do. A good night, and a do-

this-or-that; that was all we got for a while. There were some nights when the cold air outside was darkest and the fire was brightest when Papa would stay up staring at the flames, eyes lit with consuming hatred. Then he would clutch at his head with both hands and his shoulders would shake. He'd just sit there, sobbing, as the fire hissed from its hearth. It frightened Lily, young as she was, and it frightened me, too. I pretended nothing was wrong so I could be strong for Lily. I just had to be, or our little family would fall apart.

Then Papa would stop crying, his cold grey eyes would close, and he would sleep there in a chair next to the fire. So I would take Lily by her thin little arms and take her to bed, and I would go to bed too, only I wouldn't sleep. I would lie in bed and look up at the dusty ceiling and wonder where Mama was now. Eventually I would sigh and roll over and try to sleep, with my eyes screwed up tight to fend off the darkness. But just as I would be drifting off, with white-hot visions of flames lapping at my mind, I would hear Lily crying. The sound of her breathless wailing always cut like a knife through my shallow nightmares, pulling me out before I could drown. And I would crouch by her bed in the dry, parched darkness and sing Mama's song.

"Hush little darlin', don't you cry,
Mama's gone away for another night.

Hush little darlin', don't look so sad,
Mama loves you so and she misses you bad."

After that, Lily would nod off, and her gentle snoring would hold off my dreams until the dawn finally cast its multi-hued light over the sandpaper morning.

Sitting on my bed, I gazed out at the vibrant sunrise, watching the fiery light spill into the horizon and stain the sky with fire. The light of the sun gleamed like liquid flame, licking out across the heavens and dyeing the pink clouds a deep, layered crimson. The scene too closely resembled a great fire in the sky, bringing chilling remembrances of the night we lost Mama rushing back. And with those memories returned the agonizing knowledge that it was all my fault.

I always remembered how dark it was that night. It was one of the things that would always stick with me, through the rest of my life. Every shadow so alive, in stark contrast to the brilliance of the heavens...

The sky stretched out before me, endless, glittering with lengths of twinkling stars. I sighed, and the lantern flame hissed and guttered.

"What's on your mind, darling?" Mama's quiet voice filled the relatively chilly air, dancing over the silence to reach my ears. I shook my head and leaned on Mama, pointing a

glowing white hand at the sky. Mama smiled and nodded her head, tracing the stars with her long, slim fingers.

"That's Cassiopeia. She was a queen," Mama explained very studiously. At that moment, Lily came outside of our house, carrying last month's almond cookie biscuits in an old tin. She sat down on the rough-hewn rock steps, passing Mama and me each a cookie. I grinned with delight and crunched into the hard biscuit. Mama looked at Lily with a flicker of humor in her deep brown eyes. "My little flower, those are long stale."

Lily looked up at Mama and smiled a gap-toothed grin. "But Mama, they're almond'n yummy." She still had a habit of slurring and speaking in fractured sentences, as some young ones do. Mama and Papa thought it was impossibly adorable, but I considered it quite annoying. I grabbed a cookie biscuit, cramming it into my mouth. After swallowing, with some difficulty, I sat for a while longer with Lily and Mama, allowing my thoughts to wander. Drawing in the cold Colorado air, I looked up into the inky sky, imagining my childish dreams abandoned among the stars. I closed my eyes and saw myself spinning through unfounded, gauze-like darkness, illuminated briefly by passing moons and stars. Mama's hand on my shoulder tugged me out of my lonely thoughts. I looked around.

"Mama, where did Lily go?" I turned to her.

"Little Flower went inside to sleep," Mama said. "Perhaps we should be going to bed soon as well, Alex. It's very late." She lifted the lantern and got up. I stood and took Mama's hand, turning to follow her inside. She shooed me off in the direction of my bedroom. She walked towards the kitchen, swallowed by the soft, dry darkness. The light moved away with her, leaving me in shadows. I didn't want to go to bed and all at once the darkness seemed to come alive with malice well-disguised until now. I took quick steps toward my mama, heading after her, following the bobbing light of the lantern in the shadows of the house.

Suddenly, flame erupted in my vision, dancing over my eyes and exploding in bursts of colored light. It tripped across my senses, pounding my nerves with a white-hot, iron tread. When the blossoming flowers of tie-dyed color finally cleared from my tender eyes, I realized there was a fire in the front room. I dashed heedless toward the flames, scrambling through the kitchen. I halted, coughing and hacking as smoke affronted me. It filled the air quickly, its dark fingers searching for a way into my lungs. I dropped to the ground, crawling forward desperately, seeking Mama. Then I spotted her.

Here was the source of my nightmares, this scene from the darkest gashes of my soul. Mama was standing opposite me, beside the broken lantern, the reaching wall of flames *separating us, clawing determinedly up and out. Its claws sought purchase in our home, scouring the room for fuel. Smoke so thick that it seemed the very essence of darkness poured from the flames like oil. Mama's face was vanishing in front of me, too far to reach, as the smoke thickened. Her face had looked so glowingly white among all the smoke. I could hear Mama coughing, struggling for breath. Then the smoke obscured her; I lost my mama, and suddenly the coughing stopped. This shook me to my core, launching my limbs into motion. I stumbled, trying to force myself on, to reach Papa and warn him, to tell him Mama was in danger.*

My throat was raw and sore and I couldn't stop coughing. "Papa!" I tried to scream, but all that came out was a croak. I collapsed to the ground completely, legs and arms trembling. For a length of time unknown to me, I fought for breath. Finally, with a massive amount of effort, I took a sooty gulp of air and screamed. Sounds in the background faded as Papa rushed in with two men who had been working with him on our generator in the barn. They pushed me from the room and dashed about, throwing dirt, going to fetch water from the well, doing whatever they could to stop the fire.

I stumbled outside, hacking. I wanted to help Papa save Mama, but I couldn't breathe or think. I sank to the ground outside as the voices, the yelling, and the crackling fire faded into a muffled whisper. I awoke some time later, still coughing and with a pounding headache. My gaze felt empty and lifeless. I turned to look at our home as vicious black smoke poured from it in waves. The oily darkness obscured the stars, smudgy and black against the sky. My limbs felt useless and watery. I lay helplessly on the ground, dead to the world, like Mama surely was.

And I wept.

I cried at the memory, the bitter tears running trails over my skin. I sobbed for what felt like a long time, my body shaking thinly with pain. Finally my cries subsided and I tried to stop my hands from trembling. Remembering Mama's death was only hurting me. Obviously I needed to stop thinking and start working. The fields needed all the attention they could get. Part of why I didn't mind working in the fields was the fact that I got to wear trousers instead of an everyday dress. My work clothes were stained with dirt. Nothing was ever truly clean in the dry, soil-ridden recesses of southeastern Colorado. I sauntered out to the kitchen, shaking off the violent emotions that had seized my heart with the flashback. I sniffed the air appreciatively.

Papa was cooking breakfast! He was flipping pancakes in our heavy iron skillet. Their golden brown skin was marred by bits of charred grease, blackened by the intense heat. My mouth began watering as the warm smell of well-cooked batter reached me, coupled with the sight of melted butter oozing over a stack of freshly steaming pancakes. "Pancakes!" I squealed happily. We even had store-bought syrup! I almost laughed out loud with happiness. Papa smiled at me. Except for those nights when he silently wept by the fire, Papa was the strongest person I knew. I hugged him happily.

"Why d'we get fancy syrup, Papa?" I gestured toward the table. Papa raised an eyebrow.

"Y"think this here's for you?" He said with mock severity. "Ain't for anyone but my thirteen-year old daughter!" For a moment, I stared at him in puzzlement. Lily was seven, and I was twelve... Thirteen! I was thirteen today! The nightmares had been so bad lately, I had forgotten my birthday. Suddenly I looked around, mystified.

"Papa? Where's Lily?" She loved this syrup, and she hadn't had any since before Mama left us. I pushed the thought away.

"Happy Birthday to you, Happy Birthday to you!" Lily was suddenly there, in front of me, holding a large stack of pancakes with one candle in the middle. She swayed, smiling, the flame dancing with her movement. Papa and Lily sang Happy Birthday to me and I blew out the candle, suddenly feeling significantly older. My soul felt large and airy inside me, the impending despondency I felt over Mama long forgotten. My thirteenth birthday was great. We feasted on pancakes and left off an entire hour before our day's work on the farm began. Papa, Lily and I spent that time playing checkers and laughing. We were so happy.

But that was before everything went wrong, before death came again to reach out for another victim.

CHAPTER TWO

Things progressed quietly after that. We got on with our lives, with me finally being thirteen and Lily and Papa the same as ever. Well, not entirely. I was trying to teach Lily some of the things Mama had taught me. Lily needed to know that we were very, very lucky people. We had this whole house to ourselves, without a boarder or anything. And it had *four* rooms! Me 'n Lily, we had our own little bedroom beside Papa's, and there was the kitchen and the front room. We also had a good, deep well that never ran dry like other folks' did occasionally. It made everything much easier. The city slicker that had lived in our home before us left behind an indoor toilet and running water in the kitchen. Life was very good for me and Papa and Lily. Even if we had lost Mama, we were still incredibly blessed.

I thought about my friend Sarah. Her huge family all lived together in a three-room cabin. It wasn't even made sturdy like our home was. Sarah and her three brothers shared a room; I only had to share my bedroom with Lily. At least we were both girls! I couldn't imagine what it was like for Sarah.

Her parents shared a room with her grandparents, and their family's kitchen doubled as a front room. I had spent the night with Sarah exactly once, and I didn't intend to do it again. It was much too cramped over there. We'd camped out in the kitchen, and it really wasn't very much fun. They didn't even have a checker board like we did. I'd felt bad then, living in such good conditions while Sarah and her family lived like that.

God smiled on us. On Sundays like today, Lily and I each had two nice dresses to pick from when we were getting dressed for church. Most girls my age were lucky even to have one special-occasion dress, and here I was with two! Not to mention the ribbons. Oh, the beautiful ribbons Mama gave to us. It had been Christmastime...

"Mama! Papa! Oxie!" We awoke to Lily's squealing from the front room. Lily had been calling me that for almost a year now. From her inability to form the word "Alex" had sprung "Ox" which eventually became "Oxie", and the nickname had stuck. "Come on!" She called. I opened my eyes that morning, a tired little girl. I was nine years old, and Lily was a little over three. My tiredness vanished as I heard Lily calling in excitement that Santa had come. I bolted upright, falling out of bed, and scrambled to my feet. I met Mama and Papa, who were smiling sleepily at me, in the hallway and slipped and slid into the front room. Our little tree was

decorated prettily, soft strings of berries and dried flowers woven into its branches. There was an oil-lantern behind it that cast light gleaming through its needles, sending shadows dancing around the room. It was beautiful to my young eyes that Christmas morning.

Underneath the tree sat two small packages, wrapped in pale brown paper. They were tied with bright white string. Lily and I fell upon them eagerly. I stared at the little box in my hand, blinking with wide eyes at it, preparing myself to open my Christmas present. I pulled the brown paper apart carefully, first untying the string. Then I rolled it up and re-tied it. I would use it later for something. With a deep breath, I pulled off the top of the little cardboard box. My eyes glittered in awe at what lay neatly folded inside. I lifted out the beautiful silk ribbon. I stared at it, and then at Mama's proud smile. She nodded encouragingly at me. I stroked the ribbon's soft material, admiring the beautiful lace that adorned its edges. It was a deep ruby color, and it would look perfect in my sandy hair. The lace was a mosaic of white and gold. It was the most frilly, intricate thing I had ever seen. I beamed without even meaning to. Then I folded it carefully in its box before jumping up to latch onto Mama's waist, nearly knocking her over. She made an oomph sound and laughed.

"Do you like it?" She asked, even though she knew. I squeezed my hands together tightly and nodded.

"Mama, it's so pretty! Where did you get it?" Then it occurred to me that Lily had to have gotten one, too. I turned to my younger sister and found her seated firmly on the floor, beaming up at us with the ribbon woven clumsily into her dark brown hair. She clapped her hands and squee'd with delight.

"Mama! So purdy!" Her ribbon was simpler, but no less beautiful; it was a dark sapphire silk, with golden embroidered edges. The ribbon was bright, shimmering almost. The gifts were both lovely. Lily would care more for hers when she grew older.

"Thank you, Mama. Thank you, Papa." We said simultaneously, although Lily's words were softer and less formed than mine were. Papa looked down at us with mischievously sparkling eyes.

"What, did y'all think that's all we got for ya?" Then, from behind his back, he produced two beautiful white peppermint sticks, their smooth surfaces gleaming in the lantern-light. I had seen these very candies in the window of the general store many a time; never had I had the selfishness to ask for one. Once Papa had surprised Lily and me with one half a stick for the both of us to share, and we'd given some to Mama and Papa then. Now, we each had one… I had one all to myself. Lily took her peppermint stick and greedily began to gnaw on the edges. I looked on in horror. How could she be *eating it so fast? I sat there licking mine, savoring it slowly. We closed our eyes in rapture as the sweet candy melted in our mouths. It was soft and creamy, but solid at the same time. I would never understand how peppermint was made to be so... delicious. Lily and I made the treats last for a few days, but I am partly ashamed to say that we ate them fairly quickly.*

We wore the beautiful silk in our hair the next Sunday to our little church by the creek bed. Mama wove it expertly into my hair as she braided it. I felt like a princess with my hair shining and brushed and that perfect ribbon on my head like a crown. All that day, I was careful not to ruin my beautiful hair. I did not run and play like Lily did. Instead I stayed with Mama, holding her hand. I held myself like a grown-up, sitting quietly in the pews, making sure the people behind me could see my lovely silk ribbon. That Christmas and the Sunday after were some of the happiest days I spent with Mama. And some of the last.

Looking back on Christmas, I remembered why I'd loved Mama so much. She was such a giving person. It made her so happy to make other people happy. I smiled in the mirror at myself as I combed my hair. I had learned how to weave the ribbon in beautifully; but I wasn't as good at it as Mama had been, and Papa had no skill whatsoever for styling hair. Once he tried to braid it, and it took me forever to get the ribbon untangled. I could see him now, his tongue stuck out and his eyes squinty as he fiddled with my hair. I remembered how he slapped my hand away and I giggled to myself. Snapping back to the present, I realized that my braid wasn't as neat or tight as Mama's, but the ribbon made it pretty enough. I looked at my reflection. The dress was of simple-looking green homespun cotton. It hung down without any semblance of curve; the dress was entirely without body, and that suited me just fine. It was comfortable, at least, and that I was grateful for. There was a latticed design in white over the bodice and that made it good enough for church. I tidied myself in the reflection, tucking back stray hair and straightening my dress. Then I washed my face and stepped back to look at my reflection. It was acceptable.

I went to help Lily get ready, and soon we were on our way to church. We walked there, seeing as the town was small and it wasn't too far. "Be careful not to get dirt on your shoes, Lily," I cautioned her, even though I knew it wouldn't do much good. We walked and walked. Lily skipped along happily, holding my hand and dragging me along with her. Papa kept a wary eye on us. Lily was singing and looking around, her head swiveling in all directions, her bright eyes taking in the world. I smiled at her and her joy in life. She tripped over a rock, but used me to catch herself, giggling. She nearly pulled me down in the process, and I scuffed my shoes with soil. I tried to give her a hard look – after all, she'd almost tossed me into the dirt! – But my sternness melted when I saw her little face twisted into a frown.

"Oxie!" She cried, tugging at me. "Oxie, are you okay?" I looked into her exaggerated features, her brown eyes wide with worry, and I felt my anger slip away. I took her hand, smiling. She was such a funny little kid.

"I'm fine. Let's skip!" We went hop-skipping right up into the church. I didn't care so much about my hair as I did that far-off day after Christmas; I cared more about Lily now. She was my whole life. Sure, I loved Papa; I loved him very much. But I cared for Lily the way a mother hen cares for its chicks. She was my little sister. Papa could take care of himself, but Lily was another matter. She was so young, so fragile. I was terrified of losing her. But while she was the person I took care of, my burden, she was also my strength. To me, Lily represented all that was innocent and sweet in the world, all the goodness and life that existed. She was light. It would destroy me to lose her.

As we followed Papa into the little sanctuary of the church, I flashed back to right after we had lost mama. It still hurt my heart to remember Lily's little face all red and puffy from crying, and the broken-hearted wailing she'd put up when we told the little girl that her Mama was never coming back. I didn't want to see her like that ever again. I was going to care for her now.

Church was good that day. It was a simple service – just the Pastor talking – but the message was powerful. Pastor Ross spoke about healing and forgiveness. He made a point that we must always forgive ourselves before we try to take on life. His words seemed to release a wicked knot inside me, at least part of it, anyway. I felt some relief from the pain I'd felt so long that I'd forgotten it was there. Forgive myself. I would work on that.

The service ended after communion and I was just about to follow Papa and Lily out the door when a loud voice next to me sang, "Hi!" I turned, wondering, and saw a little boy with a shock of bright red hair standing next to me. He had a spray of light freckles across the bridge of his nose and on his cheeks, and the brightest, most cheerful honey eyes I'd ever seen. He was grinning in a friendly way and he stuck out his hand and grabbed mine, shaking it side to side.

"Now, why d'you do that?" I asked curiously. He stopped shaking my hand and put his hands on his hips.

"I'm Willard, Willie for short, please. An' why not?" He asked brightly, looking at me with open eyes.

That stumped me. He was right. Why not? I smiled at him, "I'm Alexandria, Alex for short if y'don't mind," and shook his hand again… side to side.

CHAPTER THREE

Life always seemed better after a relaxing Sunday. Waking up bright and early Monday morning, I tied my hair up and prepared to work my chores. Just as I was heading out to the barn to get the chicken feed, I was startled by a loud, "Hi!" I jumped and whirled around. I sagged in relief and rolled my eyes at the same time.

"Gracious, Willie, you scared the stuffing out of me!" I exclaimed, marveling at how a boy with such bright hair could sneak up on me in such an open place. "How'd you do that, anyhow? Where'd you come from?" I asked, sucking in my cheeks in thought. I imagined him prancing on fairy toes across the open ground, with a face on him like a mischievous miggun. I didn't know what a miggun was, but the words sounded good together in my head, so I kept them up there for good measure.

"All's I did was walk right'n up to you, real slow like," said Willie, grinnin'.

"Did not," I said in disbelief. "How is that? You just walked on up here? And I didn't see you at all?" He nodded secretively, darting his eyes around in his head.

"You was turned 'way from me, tho'," he admitted, screwing up his freckly nose and swiping at it with the back of one pale hand.

"Why are you so pale, Willie?" I asked. "You're always out and about in the sun, leastaways I am, so shouldn't you be darker like the rest of us?"

Willie stuck his hands in his pockets and sauntered around me in a circle. "Why's would I give up on my compleyeckshun to be all burnt-up like you lot?" He sniffed dramatically, as though his paleness were his own thought and choice. I raised my eyebrows. Now, Mama hadn't had time to teach me everything, and lots of what I'd learned had faded since then, but I knew *compleyeckshun* wasn't a word. I searched my mind for the right one.

"Do you mean complexion, Willie? Where'd you learn a word like that?"

He stared down his nose at me. "Ain't that what I said, then? Complecksh... compleckshon." He shook his head as if getting rid of an irritating insect. "Anyhows, I learnt it right proper in the schoolhouse, back when I took m'courses wit' them other kids," he said proudly. "I a'membered it just now on accounta it bein' such a long word for *skin*. I always thought that were odder'n anythin' under the sun, so I did," he said. I burst out laughing.

"Sure you're not more odd, Willard?" I said. He stuck his tongue out at me and then ran a distance away to a nearby flowering tree. He flopped on his back in the dirt, making an angel shape. I laughed at him and turned back to the barn. I was young and happy to have found such a carefree friend, even if he popped up outta nowhere, sometimes.

The rest of my day passed by uneventful. I toiled in the fields as usual, for it was mid-May; the last frost having since passed. We had to begin planting our corn, and we'd been tilling and fertilizing the fields for awhile now. I dusted off my hands on my clothes, then put my palms on my hips and surveyed the fields. Our farm was really small; only 160 acres. An older boy from town, Joey, worked the fields for us in exchange for a small percentage of the crops. We didn't see him often, but his work was always done. Papa and the other farmers around helped each other out quite a bit. They traded chores and whatnot sometimes when somebody needed a hand. Papa also had a business relationship with a nearby farmer who let us borrow his truck to cart our crops into town for selling. He used our farm equipment when he needed it, and we got to use his truck.

Papa had taught me everything he knew about the fields. Papa worked a lot more than I did, but I did my best. Today I'd finished tilling and laid down some manure. We should be ready to plant in a few days, and the hard work would only continue from there. I nodded my head proudly, satisfied with my work.

I was tired, but supper had to be started. Papa had gone into town over an hour ago; he should be back any time. Hopefully he'd have some interesting news to impart. He always brought back news of what was happening around town and in nearby states. My stomach growled, and I glanced down at it. Mama had always had the *best* recipe for stew. It was the potato-and-leek-and-beef-and-garlic-and-everything-else kind of stew. I swallowed, starting to make myself really hungry. I should have gone in and gotten the water boiling, and added the potatoes and onions for the broth. I loitered on the doorstep, though, reminiscing.

Mama taught me to always let some of the potatoes boil into the broth for a long time, until they weren't there anymore. I smiled to myself, remembering. I had always wondered where the first potatoes went. Then Mama explained that they got smaller as the broth got thicker, until, poof! They were gone. I shook myself and clomped into the house. I went back to change clothes before supper.

"Papa!" I called, as I heard the front door swing shut. "You home yet?"

"No," he answered. "I ain't done at the market. I reckon I could be home in time for dessert."

Rolling my eyes, I wandered into the front room. I decided to give him a report on what I'd done.

"The crops look good. I tilled the last of the soil after you left today, on the far half of the corn field. It took me a right long time to do, too, on account of that ground being so hard." Papa looked at me worriedly and I backtracked quickly. I hated seeing worry on his face. He had enough to think about without me rambling on about nothin'.

"What I mean is, it's just been a bit drier than usual out, is all. We haven't had a spot of rain in quite a while." I winced mentally. I wasn't making him feel better. "Anyhow, I'm sure it'll rain soon, I reckon. I tilled the soil anyways; it just took a bit longer." I finished ungracefully.

Papa looked at me from narrow gray eyes, deep in thought. His shoulders were tensed up like he was thinking about something, probably why his eldest daughter was going on about the fields when she should be cooking supper. Then he looked at the floor and ran a frustrated hand through his graying hair. I frowned. Papa wasn't so old. He shouldn't have gray hair yet, should he? Only the elders in the town had that. Papa wasn't an elder! Maybe it was a bad sign. Maybe Papa's time was running out. I shook my head, horrified with the way my thoughts were heading.

"Alex, d'you hear me?" Papa was staring at me, squinting. I widened my eyes, wondering how long I'd been standing there looking at him like a mute fool.

"I, uh, no sir." I offered, wincing.

He sighed. "I said, we gonna have t'make some changes 'round here," He hesitated. "You's always goin' down to the market to sell our extra eggs n'milk durin' the week." I nodded at him, wondering where exactly he was going with this.

"Well," he said, "Things gotta change." I blinked, thinking about my daily chores.

"What do you mean, Papa?" I asked, wringing my hands.

"We gonna sell off some cows, which means there ain't gonna be no more extra milk. The eggs keep better'n milk ever did, which means less o' that goin' to town for you," he offered. "In fact, you won't needa go to market at all, 'cause I can take them eggs in w'me when I go. As for the cows, we'll take 'em over to the Yates farm for 'em to slaughter. I just talked to Bill this morn', and they agreed to take part o' the meat as pay." He shook his head sadly. "We just ain't able t'feed 'em anymore, Alex. Like you said, it ain't rained in so long."

My initial reaction was one of fear — if times were so tough that we had to sell our animals, what would we fall back on when the rest of our food was gone? 'Course, less cows meant less milking, right? I realized it wouldn't be so bad. This would make a big difference in my chores. We already did lots of work in the fields, mostly together. I preferred working with Papa; it was less difficult and more enjoyable with another person alongside you. I used to go into the market and sell, though, about two or three times a week. I would have more time to work the fields now that I wasn't doing that. We followed the Bible's rule and tried to rest on Sundays, but seeing as times were getting tougher, we couldn't always do that. Before Mama left us, I always assumed Lily would be helping in the fields when she got older. I imagined her and me and Papa, working in the hot Colorado sun together. But then Mama went away, and Lily took over the housework best she could.

I had to help Papa show Lily how to do lots of things, but she picked 'em up pretty quick and soon enough we'd all settled into our routines. Lily kept the house running real smooth, even though our electricity usually only worked right in the mornings or mid-day. She learned to prioritize and finish what few chores had to be done with power in the mornings. Me and Papa kept food on the table and money in the budget. But as of late, things had slowed down and times were getting even tougher. Looking at Papa now, I tried to listen. I shook my head in disbelief. We were going to sell some of the cows. Papa was looking anxiously at me, and once again I jolted myself out of my doomed reverie.

"Alex, y'alright w'all this?" I hesitated. At that moment, Lily ran in.

"Papa!" She squealed. "You're home!" Then she turned to me. "Oxie, are you done working today?" She beamed her gap-toothed grin. A pair of scrubbed trousers was slung over her shoulder, a remnant of the laundry she'd obviously left off doing to talk to us. Lily was a strong little girl. It was my turn to be strong. I was afraid, but who wouldn't be? Things would work out just fine, they always did. Us selling off some cows didn't mean we were going under. Papa was trying to keep us afloat in a drowning time. I didn't need to make holes in the boat.

"Hi, Lil Flower," I said to my sister. She turned to talk to Papa as my thoughts drifted. I'd adopted the pet name like Mama used to call her, 'cept Mama said "Little". I preferred Lil. It was part of her name.

Tugging her ponytail, I said, "Go finish your chores, Lily. I'll get supper started in a bit." Lily swatted my hand away and darted off.

I turned back to Papa, confident and feeling better about everything. Seeing the pride in his gray eyes, the pride he felt for his daughters, I knew he was reassured as well.

"We'll adjust just fine, Papa," I said surely. "Sounds like a fine idea to sell off some cattle, as long as you bring back a new radio tomorrow for my room!" He snorted, relieved, and went on to his room to change. I turned to start supper, my mind wandering. It was a long running joke we had, the new radio. Papa and I were out one day on the town, and we saw one of them spoiled-rich families shopping in the General store. Their little daughter was turning her nose up at the fanciest radio the town had to offer. She'd said quite clearly and loud enough for the whole shop to hear,

"Mother, I don't *want* this one. It's too old. Can't we find a better one in the city?" Her mother didn't pay her any mind, and that didn't sit right with the girl at all. "Mother!" She'd shrieked. The word sounded so odd, so formal in her mouth. Like she was yelling at a servant instead of her own mama.

The woman looked up from her important dealings with the store owner and begged, "Katherine, *please,* darling. Do be quiet. Mommy's trying to speak with a grown-up." This set the little girl off into a crying fit.

"Mother doesn't love me," She wailed. "Mother wishes I was dead." Her cries had echoed in my ears.

The woman had turned very quickly and pleaded with her daughter, "Please, Katherine, dear! I'll buy you a dozen radios for your room when we get back from vacation, just give Mother a moment, darling! Don't cry. My beautiful little sugar blossom, please, dear," she cooed. The little girl fell silent with a sullen sniff as her mother handed her a bag filled with sugary candies.

"Vacation?" The girl had muttered. "This daft little town is more like a punishment."

Looking back on the incident always made me feel annoyed and sad at the same time. The mother had simply brushed off her snobby daughter with bribes; it seemed so informal and lonely. The rich little trio had left a week later, bound for the city and their unfortunate lives. I grimaced at the thought of being born into such circumstances.

As often as I remembered, I thanked God that I'd had such a wonderful Mama and for my amazing Papa. I thanked Him for teaching me how to work, for showing me the joy in earning your life. I couldn't imagine living in the dirty bustle of a city, around the cramped spaces and throngs of people. Leastaways that was what Mama had always described it as.

Mama had a foggy past that she very seldom spoke of. She didn't like the city at all, and I couldn't quite figure why we never knew much about where she came from, about her parents. My grandparents, the ones I never got to meet. Papa's parents passed on when he was a little boy, and he'd been shipped to the town and grown up with his only living relative nearby. Papa was a pure-bred farm boy, that much I knew for sure. His book learning was near nonexistent. I'd never asked where exactly he came from, but I knew it had to be someplace else because of how unique his accent was. Come to think of it now, he sounded a lot like Willie. I wondered if they'd come from similar places.

When Mama moved to the town, he'd fallen head over heels in love with her. "'An' when I finally got m'self convinced to talk to'er, yer ma fell for me too, I'd like t'think'," I finished the story aloud, badly mimicking Papa's accent, thinking of all the times I'd heard it told. Mama always laughed at that part and rolled her eyes. My parents had a real happy story. They worked hard to build a life together, and wasn't it a prosperous one. Full of joy and laughter.

What treasures I considered those to be, joy and love and laughter and family. How could even a dozen radios compare to my Mama's love for my Papa? I shook my head and focused on the stew I was making. I couldn't start thinking about what we lost when Mama went away, not now. I was too full of happiness for my family, and a determination to make things work, no matter what it took. Things would get better.

As I chopped potatoes and tossed them into the thickening broth, my mind began to wander once again. I wondered about Willie. I hadn't seen his parents at the service that morning. Didn't they believe? Was Willie alone in his faith? No, I assured myself. People didn't just *not* believe in God, not around here. Why would you want to make it worse for yourself, thinking we're alone on the planet? Besides, proof of God was everywhere – the stuff God had created for us.

Flowers, the wind, the rain, the very act of laughing. How could all that be an accident? We recognized His handiwork, we did. I came to the conclusion that Willie's mama and papa must have just been busy, is all. Maybe he had a sick brother or sister. Skipping service one Sunday wasn't a big deal if something was going on at home. At least they'd allowed Willie to go on without them.

I hated missing church; going to service always made my week a little brighter. Some of God's strength always seeped out of Pastor's words and filled my heart with iron will, with determination and confidence and good intention. I always felt like God took the service and used it like a medicine to heal the sick and wounded at heart. Going to church had sure healed me after losing Mama. It took a long time, sure, and I was broken inside for such a while after my body started functioning right without me. I had learned to accept condolences with the right answers, to make people feel good for caring and to accept their offers of prayers and friendly check-ups on me and my family.

After a few months, people left us alone, to grieve in silence. That was the way around here. The community came up to you real close right after an incident, to offer their support and make sure you knew they were there. But after a while, after they knew that *you* knew you weren't alone, they backed off so you could breathe – and cry – in silence. It had always been the way around here.

Town was a family in itself. We all took care of one another, for the most part. Never did a broken heart go without a kind word to soothe it. People couldn't always spare monetary help; we were a real tight-budget town, with most families living day-by-day and without a dime extra. However, some folks would give you the coat off their back if you needed it. Nobody ever walked alone spiritually, either, if they knew where to go for help. My family spared a thought and a worry when we could, and so did most folks in return.

Before Mama left us, I'd always wondered at the idea of losing somebody so close to you. The image did not suit me at all; losing my Mama would be losing part of me, and losing my Papa would be the sun forgetting to warm the earth. So when Mama did go away, the town's support meant a lot. They came together to care for us, kinda like a big old smothering group hug. Being held while you grieve means a lot.

I sniffed appreciatively, my thoughts coming back to the present. Supper was just about done. The stew smelled wonderful; big chunks of beef, well done; mushy onions and potatoes that had melted half-way into the broth; peas and carrots and corn that were steeped through with the overall flavor of the stew. It was an old family recipe, and had always been my favorite.

"Supper's ready!" I hollered. I started ladling the stew into big earthenware bowls, aware of my family's voracious appetite. Even Lily would eat like a ravenous dog after a full day like today. I ripped off chunks of bread from a fresh loaf and placed them next to each bowl, scattering golden crumbs everywhere. I waited, and soon enough Lily and Papa showed up, taking their places with delighted words for my skill. I lapped up the praise, glad to have such a delicious supper in front of me. It was a hearty meal, one of the healthiest of our usual diet. Before we dug in, we joined hands for a prayer.

Lily began, "Lord, bless our food that Oxie made us. Help us grow big and strong and work hard for you always, Daddy. Thank you for Oxie's great meal and her and Papa's hard work outside and Papa's strength for us. Thank you for the meat and the potatoes and the leeks and the carrots and peas and corn, and thank you for the bowls we have God, that we don't have to eat out of the pot like Isaiah and his family," I marveled at Lily and her innocent prayer.

She was so young-minded, so pure. Rambling on about the day. "And thank you for Alex being so pretty, Daddy! Can I be pretty like her when I grow up? Thank you for making Oxie look like Mama, so I never forget her! And thank you for our meal! Amen!"

I looked cautiously at Papa, wondering if Lily's words had made his eyes water like they'd almost mine. He looked back at me, and suddenly we both just burst out laughing. It was great to be alive, to have her light in our presence. We ate with a will and an essence of life that night. Never had I been so thankful for our life together since the accident as that day. We were together, after all. What a reason to live.

CHAPTER FOUR

"Lily!" I yelled. "Come on out here!" Lily skidded into the front room, eyes bright with excitement. We were both wearing the best of our everyday clothes. Our Sunday dresses were kept nice for church and very special occasions. Lily was in a little flowery white dress that Mama had made long ago for me. My dress was made from an old flour bag, printed with bright blue blossoms. It had been a gift from some of the older ladies at church who'd noticed my dresses getting small on me. I felt an uncomfortable turning in my stomach as I realized that making dresses for us should be up to me now that Mama was gone.

"Is it time to go, Oxie?!" Lily cried, bouncing on the balls of her feet. I laughed and leaned against the wall behind me.

"Just about, Lily. We gotta eat some breakfast, and then we'll go on by the fork in the road to meet Willie, and then it's on to the Founder's Day Festival!" Lily skipped around me in a circle. Her dark brown hair bounced with her. This would be her first Founder's Day Festival since long before Mama died.

We used to go as a family, and, well, once Mama was gone... it really hurt too much, for too long. I really hadn't expected to go today, but Papa insisted. He said that since I was gonna be working so hard around here, we deserved a day to relax.

It was Friday, exactly thirty-four years from the day our little town was founded. Papa was gonna be working here today alone, so that we could go on to the festival. He said that I should take Lily and Willie on to the Town Square to enjoy ourselves; He even gave us each three pennies to spend. I was really worried about how much money we had, so I quietly left my pennies behind on the counter. He'd see it later and put it back where it belonged. But I kept the six cents for Willie and Lily.

I asked Papa what we'd do if Willie already had some spending money, but he just shook his head and declared to give it to him anyway. Willie had become a real friend around here. He showed up at the oddest of times and helped out with the work. Privately I thought he must not have much money at home, 'cause his mama gave him permission to eat supper over here an awful lot. I think Papa picked up on that, too.

Maybe that was why he'd provided a few cents for Willie. I was proud of my papa. Many folks would think giving kids spending money far too frivolous, like Mama used to say about the rich folk. But Papa believed in rewarding somebody for lots of hard work, and we'd all three been at it for quite a few weeks now. That was part of why we didn't mind about the supper. Willie worked hard with us. We had plenty big portions, and cutting off a bit of each of ours, we had enough to share. I wondered sometimes at how his mama and papa got on without him. Maybe he had lots of siblings, so a little guy like him wasn't needed. It didn't make a whole lot of sense, though, 'cause if Willie's family was low on money, how could they spare a worker? 'Course, I wasn't complaining, and I wasn't about to question my bright little friend. He made working a whole lot more fun. I was sure that whatever reason his folks had for letting him help us, it had to be a good one.

Lily and I went on our way after shoveling down some hearty oats for breakfast. I'd mixed them with preserved corn from last season, and some dried apple slices from the Market. They were real good for us and a great start for the day. Mama always said that the better a breakfast, the better a day. I believed her. Lily and I walked side by side down the road, headed for the fork. We took to meeting Willie there pretty often. He never invited us to his home, and we never asked why. Maybe he was ashamed of it.

"Willie!" I called, as we neared the fork in the road. "Y'here yet?" A bright red shock of hair popped up from behind a tree. Willie scrambled up from where he'd been leaning against the trunk.

"Here yet?" He grunted questioningly. "Been here goin' on *ages*, wonderin' what happened t'you lot!" He said, pretending to yawn. I snorted and threw a punch at him. He ducked, grinning.

"How d'ya do, Lil Monster!" He sang at Lily. He'd taken my pet name and adapted his own. Nuisance.

I shook my head as he picked Lily up and swung her onto his back. I marveled at how such a tiny boy could pick her up like that. He looked so scrawny. But then, I reflected, working in the fields with me was sure to have put some muscles on him. He turned to me.

"C'mon, Alex, let's git on t'the square!" His bright honey eyes were cheerful as they danced all around, taking in our path. He began to shuffle down the road with Lily on his back. I laughed and darted to catch up with them, joining the happy parade. As we got closer, Lily jumped down and we ran the rest of the way to Main Street. Once we got there, we broke apart in awe. The dreary, dusty corner had been transformed into a bright, festive place. Red and blue streamers were tied to the lampposts, fluttering in the breeze. We all wandered straight past some of the booths that people had set up.

Willie pointed. "Sack toss! C'mon, guys, let's go!" He broke into a run and Lily and I scrambled to catch up. We skidded to a halt at the booth. Willie panted instructions to us in front of Miss Sally Obadiah.

"I wanna be apart o' Lily and Alex's team," He said proudly, gesturing at us.

Miss Sally smiled at him, the corners of her aged brown eyes crinkling. "Sorry love, but it's two to a team. Why don't you go with the little one and I'll step in as Alex's partner?" I smiled happily. Miss Sally was a part-time teacher at the schoolhouse, and one of the loveliest old ladies I knew. We assembled into our teams and got ready to toss the little brown sacks at our targets.

While we were playing, I noticed a group of school kids gathered at the corner, whispering and pointing at us. I tried to keep my mind on the game but missed quite a few times. That lot was distracting. Willie seemed to notice them too. He nervously scratched his head and said he had to use the bathroom. We paused our game and Lily told Miss Sally how things were going at home with our "lessons". I tried to teach Lily as much as I could about what Mama had showed me with arithmetic, etiquette, and reading, but it got hard with all the bustle of work. Especially recently. Times were getting tougher. I had begun to think that was Papa's favorite phrase, "Times are getting tougher." He said it a lot.

I noticed the end of the group of kids disappearing around the corner of the General Store. Willie was gone, too. Something nagged at me in the back of my mind. I excused myself and followed the group around the store. As I rounded the corner, my eyes narrowed in anger. The group was surrounding Willie and pushing him around. I moved closer, into hearing distance.

"...freaky little snowman! What a pale creature you are, t'be sure," they laughed. My blood stirred with anger and thickened with sickness. They were making fun of him because of how he *looked*? Shame for my generation overtook me like a wave, and for a moment I was astounded by their cruelty. Then I moved.

Working in the fields had made me a good deal stronger and broader in the shoulders than most of these weaklings. They looked to be about Willie's age. They were sneering and prodding and pushing him around. I bulled my way into the center of the group, pulled him from their grasp, and hissed out a retort, sharper than Papa's pickaxe that we used when the field ground was frozen.

"Who do you lot think you are?" I snarled. They bounced back from me, staring. Willie spit blood from his lip. I became further enraged to see the damage they'd done to his face. Scratches, cuts and bruising. These were *kids*. Willie pulled away from me.

"They was jus' jokin' around, is all," he muttered. I stared at him.

"They weren't joking," I said slowly. I looked at them, my expression cold. "You are pathetic." I said slowly. They sneered at me, scoffing, exchanging glances with one another. Fire stirred in my eyes. "Who do you think you are? Pathetic, you who bother another because of how he looks!" I spat. It was times like these when my schooling came back to me, and all the proper words Mama taught me boiled to the top of my brain.

"T'is only a heartless fool who looks in the mirror and sees a creature better than any other," I quoted. Mama had always loved those words, but only just now was I beginning to understand them firsthand. They sure were fancy words.

"What relevance makes you more beautiful than the soul? What changing feature describeth your perfection?" The group shook their heads and glanced at one another, totally confused. I fought off the sudden urge to laugh because it was clear that they had no idea what was happening. I took the chance to shove one of them over and they scattered, terrified. Then they took off running, back toward the fair. I helped Willie dust himself off. He wouldn't look at me.

"Willie," I said softly. "How long have they been picking on you?" He sighed and wiped blood from under his eye, where his cheek was split.

"Long's I can remember, I reckon." He straightened and tried to look me in the eye, but the depth of sadness in my gaze seemed to break him, and he drooped like one of Mama's dying sunflowers.

I tugged on his arm. "C'mon, let's get back to the others. We have a game to finish." He smiled half-heartedly and we turned around. There I saw Lily watching us calmly, hand-in-hand with Miss Sally. I squinted. Lily said something quickly to Miss Sally, and then she took off running around her, toward the group of bullies. Willie and I exchanged a glance and hustled to catch up.

As we rounded the corner, again, we both stopped dead. The group of kids was surrounding someone... Terror filled my veins. Lily was even smaller than Willie. If they'd so much as bruised her...

"Why?" Lily's clear little voice rang out. I was closer now. I could see their expressions, and the little boys were puzzled.

"Why d'you pick on Bubba?" Her words were soft and partially unformed.

The boy who seemed to be the leader opened his mouth, but no words came out. He glared and then tried again.

"Coz he looks all pale and scrawny, like some kind o' sickly little thing!" He drawled.

"Gracious, you do sound right dumb when you speak, don't you?" I muttered self-righteously to myself. Then I paid my attention back to Lily. Her little hands were on her hips.

"So you pick on my Bubba 'cause he's prettier than you?" She squeaked. "Well I like his hair and his freckles! They're the color of the sunset!" With that, she spit at the feet of the boys and flounced away. Their outraged and embarrassed expressions coupled with Lily's behavior were too much for me. I burst out laughing.

"Look at those fools; they can't make out which way to turn now!" I laughed. Willie was standing quietly next to me. I looked at him and smiled a soft sort of smile. Lily reached him and jumped up on him.

He caught her and said, half laughing, half crying, "Thanks, Lil Monster. Couldn'ta said it better m'self."

Lily just grinned, "Bubba's more special than all of them combined. Daddy wanted you bright like your spirit on the inside, so he gave you a happy face and happy hair." She smiled innocently as she patted his hair and jumped down.

I told Willie later that Lily meant God by "Daddy". Willie looked at me, sniffing, and as he faltered, I knew he wanted to collect himself. So I grabbed Lily and gave her the three pennies Papa had promised her. She took them happily. I pointed at a candy booth.

"Pick out something that'll make you real sugared-up," I smiled. Lily clapped her hands and skipped away. I watched her bouncing brown hair and dusty white dress as she skipped away. I looked at Willie, and three tears fell from his eyes and plowed a path through the light dust and blood on his face. He sniffed and swiped at his nose with a pale, freckle-bound hand. He spoke with a muffled voice, eyes on the ground.

"That sister of yourn is a real charmer, y'know that? Them boys better watch out when she gets older. You and I, we... we gotta make sure they treat 'er right." I shook my head, grinning.

"I think Lily'll have something to say herself if they don't treat her right!" He laughed at that and finally looked at me, bright honey eyes recovering their usual sparkle.

"I'm glad we're friends, Willie." I said softly.

He smiled and gestured at the fair. "Race ya t'the egg toss!"

CHAPTER FIVE

It was too quiet. I awoke, blinking, startled awake by the lack of noise. I lay in bed a moment, listening, straining my ears to hear anything... but there was nothing.

I sat upright quickly then, a very light fear beginning to stir in my heart. I felt the fear spread to my arms and throat. Normally I would have been hearing the radio in the kitchen, the stovetop sizzling as Papa cooked breakfast. I sniffed the air. It seemed my only companion was dust.

I leapt upright and padded hesitantly into the kitchen. I looked around, but nobody was there. The whole kitchen, the whole *house*, it seemed, was empty. Feeling the worry creep up the back of my throat, I tiptoed quickly into the front room, afraid of what I might see. Ice cold adrenaline, shot through with panic, dumped into my veins. Papa was sitting on the floor, looking down, and his face was blank and empty. I couldn't see what was in front of him. The dusty old sofa that we'd been given after the fire consumed our furniture sat in my way. I walked farther into the room, fear making me jittery.

You haven't seen Lily today; you haven't heard Lily today. Where's Lily? Where's Lily?

The thought was pounding in my head, roaring over my pumped-up senses. I came around the furniture as if in slow motion, then stopped in bitter shock when I took in the whole scene. Lily was lying sprawled on the floor, her face deathly pale, an undertone of green seeming to adorn her features. My heart stopped. Everything was in slow motion.

"Papa," I whispered. He was sitting there next to her, holding her hand. He dragged his flickering eyes up to me, and the empty look in them, the absolute despairing image of hopelessness in his gaze, froze my soul. His voice was devoid of all emotion; it was the raspy, ragged murmur of a lost man.

"She threw up. She's gonna die. I'm gonna lose her." He was looking down, and then his empty eyes were on me again. He tilted his head to one side. Papa opened his mouth, his lip quivering, drawing in a tortured breath as if it pained him. His eyelids flickered.

"You're gonna die too," he said, narrowing his starving, blank eyes. "I'm gonna lose everythin'." Then he sagged, his gaze back on the floor, exhaling as if the mere effort of speaking had exhausted him. He sat there, sighing raggedly, murmuring to himself.

I stared at him, and suddenly strength – fueled by anger – flooded into my bones. "No!" I screamed, grabbing him by the shoulders and shaking him briefly. "No," I said softly. Then I gazed down at Lily, and looked back up at Papa. His eyes had sparked the palest glimmer of sadness, of facing reality. He stood shakily.

"Help me move her," I commanded. He complied, and soon we had her lying carefully in her bed. She was breathing, at least. Her tiny chest rose and fell clearly, rhythmically. But fear still shook my limbs and turned my blood to ice because of the fire on her skin. Heat radiated from her as she whimpered and thrashed. I didn't know what to do. I turned to Papa helplessly. I saw the lost man leave, and I saw my Papa return as his eyes gained their consciousness once more. He went to summon the town doctor, and I prayed that the lost man who'd replaced my Papa for a time would never return.

An hour later, Dr. Jones reported to us in the kitchen. He was a tall, solemn man with a drawn face and high cheekbones. He had a thin, frowning mouth and deep-set eyes that always seemed sad. He didn't hesitate to let us know the truth.

"It looks a lot like meningitis," he said dully. "Fever, back pain, sore throat. All these symptoms, combined with vomiting and the stiffness in her legs, seem to point to meningitis." My eyes narrowed. *Meningitis?* The name called to mind some dim memory. Then with a jolt it came rushing back to me, the situation where I'd first heard of meningitis.

It had been a few years ago, too long ago for Lily to remember, because I could barely recall it. We lived down the road from an older couple, the Johanssons, and they had a strong young son in his thirties, named Rick, who lived with them. One day, Mrs. Johansson came down the road and called Mama to the door. She and Mama had entertained a hushed conversation outside, and then Mama had come striding back in, her face resolutely pale.

I tugged at her skirts, asking what was wrong. She looked down at me, and tender emotions flashed over her face. I saw grateful tears – and incredible sorrow – brimming in her eyes. Looking back on it then, I realized that she was glad she still had me when the next door neighbors had just lost their only son to a nameless fever later to be identified as meningitis.

CHAPTER SIX

I peered into the dimly lit room, the tin bowl I was holding sloshing its contents over the edges and onto my bare feet. "Lily?" I called quietly. "Are you awake?" A raspy voice answered me. Worry and sorrow grasped my feet with leaden hands, making my tread slow and heavy. I set the bowl of warm broth down on the wooden nightstand with a barely audible thump. The exuberance of that far-off Founder's Day seemed so unreal. So dreamlike. It seemed real and solid, at first, but gradually the reality slipped away, turning translucent, fleeting, like mist on the breeze... I shook myself out of my distressed reverie and helped Lily sit up.

"Are you okay to drink this broth, Lil? It's Mama's old recipe." Lily looked at me with tired eyes as she sat up and took the bowl. I was nearly half-way to fourteen now. Lily's illness had commandeered time, spinning it fast, then slow. The days had smeared together, like ink running on a page. She'd turned eight a week ago, but there had been no joy – and no money, for that matter – with which to celebrate. About two weeks after the first diagnosis of meningitis, Lily began to have other problems. My mind flashed back.

Lily was walking down the hallway to the front room very slowly. It was midday and she was yawning. That stuck in my mind. I was waiting for her in the doorway to the kitchen, wanting to help but holding myself back for her sake.

Scrape, thunk. Scrape, thunk.

That was when I noticed it for the first time. The way Lily walked was beginning to change. Her right leg dragged behind her, loose, floppy, starting to turn as no leg should. Bile rose in my throat.

"Lily?" I called. A moment passed before she seemed to register her name and look up at me. Fear slowed down time as I realized something far more sinister than even a fever had its hands on my sister.

Unfortunately, the doctor's original diagnosis of meningitis had been wrong. Within a few weeks, cases of polio had cropped up all over town. Then, with time, most of the other victims faded away, leaving a single lily in a field of dying flowers.

I reached over to help Lily drink the soup, my hands calloused and strong. Since Lily fell ill, Willie had always been there to lend a hand. He very nearly lived with us now. I figured that he felt invisible at his home, so he'd found a better family with us, and I couldn't be happier with it. He liked to make Lily smile and laugh when he could, and never did he complain about all the work we had to do. And work hard, we did. My hands, my arms, my torso, they were no longer thin and bony. I was covered in muscle, sinewy and tough.

Times were getting tougher.

Dust storms had begun, more than were common in the recesses of southeastern Colorado. Fancy syrup was a simple fantasy now. The broth I boiled for Lily was still full and nutritious, however. We had food enough for the family. She drank the thick broth as best she could, very slowly, exhausted by this simple maneuver. I noticed the difficulty she had swallowing. My eyes wandered down her body as she lay still, down to the twisted leg that hid like a nightmare under her blankets. The sound of her shuffling walk now pervaded my dreams, threading through my sleeping hours like a wicked lullaby I could never escape.

Lily had been left weak in the wake of her disease. The ravaging polio had left behind a twisted leg and a loose arm that could not always hold its own weight. It had left a shriveled corpse of a girl that paraded as a human. Her lungs now functioned in a broken way, as if they were meant not to catch air but dust. The coughing came and went. Her body had become a prison, holding her in with its weakness, with its insistence on sleeping the hours away. Lily could walk and talk, but she was slowly losing the will to do so when the effort cost her so much. Why leave this shadowy room when it was far easier to close her eyes? I was losing my sister to a realm of sleepiness that I was unsure she could escape from.

I prayed often for healing. God was big, and I knew he could heal Lily. I pleaded with him to spare her. I felt so much older now. So much wiser. Was wisdom pain? That was how it felt sometimes. Mama had been so wise. Why, Mama? Why did it hurt so badly? Where did the pain come from? Emotional pain, like the agony that plagued my days and nights, the piercing sickness that struck my soul in glancing blows. This pain, this illness of the mind and soul, it made my nightmares in the old days look peaceful. I longed for the comforting darkness, the blistering heat of the flames.

Instead I dreamt of gaunt, lifeless corpses, adorned with Lily's features, crawling through my dreams and clawing out my soul. I dreamt occasionally of Mama cradling me in her arms, stroking my hair and singing softly. Those dreams were what kept me going. The song Mama sang, I could never remember the words. But it was beautiful, and it gave me hope...

CHAPTER SEVEN

"Alex?" I turned from my kitchen work, toward Willie.

"Yeah, Willard?" I said. His tone was unusually serious, and it was scaring me. I tried using his full name to lighten things up, but his dark expression just deepened.

"Listen..." He began, hesitating. "I need t'do somethin' today." I watched him, brow furrowed, my gaze flicking from one of his bright honey eyes to the other.

"I gots t'go... somewhere," he started.

"You've *got* to go somewhere." I corrected him. I had been working with him on improving his grammar.

Willie ignored me. "A bit farther than th'fork in th'road, east. It's real important. But I ain't gonna have NOBODY followin' me," he said slowly, staring me down like an animal. My skin prickled as I realized how serious he was being and I wished I hadn't corrected his speech. I held my hands up in protest.

"Willie, if you say you need to go somewhere alone, I ain't gonna do anything about it. You're part of the family now," I said firmly. "So I'm hardly going to tell you, you can't go do something you say you *gotta* do, y'hear me?" He drew in a breath, raising his head as his chest inflated with air, then he ruffled his hair with skinny fingers and began to nod.

"Yeah. I got it. I just wanted t'make sure, is all, and I'm probably gonna be gone all day. So don't go lookin' for me," He said fiercely. "Can't have *nobody* followin' me, not today. And just you tell Papa and Lily that I, uh, that they needs me at home."

I wondered for a moment at this. Why hadn't he just told me the same thing? So I voiced my question aloud. "Willie, if you're all secretive about this, why is it that you didn't just tell me the same thing? I would have believed you," I insisted. He looked so sad just then, I almost had to tell him to forget it. But then his eyes flared up and he got real defensive, real fast.

"I gots to have somebody know where I'm headed! What if I didn't come back, huh? You all couldn't get on right without me," He bristled. I laughed.

"You're right, Willie. We couldn't get on right without you." He relaxed and looked down, scuffin' at the ground with one torn old work boot.

"Aw, shucks, Alex. I didn't mean to get all nasty. I just am real nervous-like, that's all. I ain't seen them in so lo–" He cut himself off, alarm flaring in his expression. Noting this, I pretended not to have heard.

"Sorry, what was that?" I asked innocently, busying myself with wiping the countertops.

He stared at me with relief. "I said, I didn't mean to get nasty. So… just know where I'm gonna be headed, okay? Past the fork, t'the east. That's all you needa know," He added bitingly. I raised my hands in defense once again.

"Relax, Willie. I'm not gonna follow you. I've got work to do around here anyhow," I added.

He looked real sorry for a moment. "I wish I could stay an' help, Alex, but today's real important-like," He insisted.

"Hey, Willie, I didn't say I needed your scrawny help today! I just got chores to do. Alex-chores. You go on. Get outta the house!" I said with mock severity, shooing at him with my hands. He grinned, his smile lighting up his serious face for a moment, and then he added one last comment, his eyes darkening briefly.

"Alex, if I ain't checked in with you guys by sunset…" He left it unfinished, and I nodded firmly.

"Got it. I'll send the hounds out if you aren't back." He shook his head, chuckling, and then took off out the back door. I watched him go, swallowing with worry. Every ounce of my being wanted to follow Willie, see what was going on. But I could hardly do that. Where on earth could he be headed? I shook my head and kept on scrubbing at the countertop. Dust sure was piling in our little home a lot more often. At that moment, Papa walked in, his cold gray eyes dull from morning-time sleepiness. He yawned, and soon enough I was yawnin' too.

"Mornin," I said through it, sounding very muffled.

He laughed and ruffled my hair. "Mornin', sleepy head."

I looked at him incredulously. "Me? Sleepy head? I've been in here a good twenty minutes longer than you've been awake, and only 'cause your yawns are contagious, you call me sleepy?" I punctuated my argument with my hands, making swirling motions to demonstrate the injustice of it all. Papa raised an eyebrow and then helped himself to some of the oatmeal that was cooling in a pot over the stove. He stopped just as he had filled his bowl, and turned to me questioningly.

"Yeah, Papa," I said, anticipating his question. "I made Lily some more broth already." I gestured toward a bowl sitting next to the stove. "It was fine from last night, I just heated it up in the pot a tad before starting the oatmeal." He closed his mouth on the unformed question, nodding.

Then he asked, "Is she gonna get up t'day?"

I hesitated, and then looked at the floor. "I don't know," I said softly. *I don't know if she wants to.*

Papa's eyes darkened and he shook his head, his graying hair looking thinner than ever.

"Part o' me... Part o'me thinks we should make 'er, make 'er get up an' walk 'round and live life. But then I a'member... the coughin'... and I couldn't abide that bein' 'cause of us."

I hesitated, mouth opening and closing as I looked for something to say. He looked at me, and I saw a shadow of the lost man that was let loose the day Lily fell ill. I felt cold anger shaking my bones, and a completely ridiculous urge to hit Papa, just for letting that lost man back into his eyes. But it passed soon enough, and I sagged against the kitchen cupboards brokenly.

"She can't be this way forever," I whispered. "Can she?" I asked, feeling haunted. "She's my little sister. The only one I got." This seemed to be all Papa could take, so he went and changed the subject.

"Speakin' of siblings, where be that young'un we took in?" He said. It was Papa's way of showing endearment to Willie, refusing to ever say his name right or acknowledge the fact that he truly belonged to a different family.

I blinked. "Willie said to tell you he's needed at his home today, actually," I said slowly. My words were true, but I wasn't telling Papa everything. I knew Willie had something to hide. I had to be convincing. Then again, as far as Papa knew, I had no reason to lie. So why shouldn't he believe me as easy as those deceptive words had fallen from my mouth? Guilt pressed against my heart.

Papa looked out the door thoughtfully.

"Oh, is he?" I was wonderin' when that family o'his would decide he was useful again." He muttered something inaudibly to himself, angrily, and I strained to hear. He blinked and looked at me, seeming to remember my presence.

"Whatcha doin', Alex? Tryin'a hear the ramblin's of a crazy man?" With that he raised one eyebrow dramatically and rumbled like a wild grizzly, lumbering toward me with rolling eyes and outstretched arms. I screamed, laughing, and darted away, toward the little hall that led to our bedrooms. I'd taken to sleeping in the kitchen nowadays, since Lily'd fallen ill. I didn't like to disturb her with my tossing and turning, nor did I feel comfortable breathing the air in there. It was so musty and ill-feeling. Turned my stomach right proper, so it did.

Papa kept after me, growling, and I passed by Lily's room, only to hear a feeble cough from inside.

"Alex?" Came a tiny voice. "I wanna play too." She coughed louder and my heart sank all the way to my feet. I hesitantly walked inside, next to her bed.

"Lil Flower, I wish you could run and play with us," I said softly.

"How about this? I promise that as soon as you're better, we'll go to that little pond in the forest and skip rocks all day," I said, my heart heavy with the iron weight of empty words.

Lily looked up at me, her sunken eyes tired and hopeful. "Like before Mama went away?" She said weakly.

I felt like I'd been pierced with a sword. Shakily, I nodded. "Yeah, Lil. Like before Mama went away." My hands felt shaky. "Listen, Lily. I gotta go now, okay? You get some more sleep now." I stumbled out of the room. Papa was at the doorway, listening with wide, troubled eyes. I exchanged one sickened look with him and then tripped down the hall, onto my sheets in the kitchen, and I began to cry. Silently, ever so silently flowed the tears. Lily still cried out in the night for her Mama, wailing hollowly for the mother who was no longer around to hear her cries. Most nights when it happened, I ran into her room and sang Mama's song, the one I'd come up with after she went away.

Then I'd have to explain to her that I wasn't Mama, 'cause most of the time she saw me coming, and her face lit up with joy, letting me see every ounce of her fragile happiness at seeing her Mama. Then it all crumbled when I reminded her who I really was. It was nights like those when I cursed myself for looking so much like Mama. I always remembered the supper when Lily prayed that she'd be, 'pretty like me', someday, like Mama. And I hated myself a little more each time.

I was just cleaning up after supper that night when the sun's rays bounced through an open window and hit a drinking glass on the counter just right, creating a rainbow of dark brilliance on the ceiling. I marveled at it and watched the beauty slip away as the sun set. Then I stood for a moment, thinking.

Sun set. Sunset...

Willie!

I breathed in so sharply that it hurt as I realized my best friend hadn't returned. I ran into our front room and shook Papa from his nap by the fire.

"Willie! It's Willie! Oh, Papa, wake up!" He startled awake and stared at me, mouth wide open in curiosity. "Papa, this morning, it wasn't late, I mean it was early, Willie said he had to go somewhere and I said it wasn't my place to stand in his way to do something he had to do 'cause he was family and he said his family needed him, no, that's not it, he said to tell you his family needed him but they didn't really, really he was off to do something important, and..." I broke off suddenly.

Seriously? Papa was actually snoring.

I panicked and was just about to yell at him to wake up when a quiet voice behind me said, "It's orright, Alex. I'm here."

I turned and saw him standing there, Willie, alive and apparition-like in the dying glow of the embers. Tears filled my eyes and I rushed to hug him. Then I pulled away in terrified, fearful anger.

"Willie, where have you been! I realized it was sunset, and I just about died from fright, you hear me?" Willie wasn't listening, though. He was staring into my eyes, but he wasn't listening. That was when I realized he was bleeding. There, on the right side of his head, his bright red hair was matted with something dark and sticky. I touched his head with one hand and it came away covered in blood. Willie faltered.

"They, just came outta nowhere... yellin'... 'orphan'..." And he toppled into my arms, unconscious.

CHAPTER EIGHT

It was long past sundown when Willie awoke, somewhere between the watches of night and morning. Papa and I had laid him down on the couch and dressed his wound. I'd sat by the fire, covered in a shaggy old blanket, keeping watch by his side. As the night wore on, I'd slipped away into the dark realms of sleep, until I sensed a change in his breathing and awoke instantly. I arose from my silent vigil and stoked the fire, until it was once again red-hot and crackling in the night, fending off the darkness. Then I watched him carefully, waiting. Soon enough he groaned and touched his head, wincing when he made contact.

"Willie?" I said quietly. He looked up at me, his face shadowed and dark. He sat up and made room for me, and I sank onto the sofa next to him. I could tell by the shame in his eyes that he remembered everything, though for what he should feel ashamed, I didn't know.

"I..." He didn't seem to know what to say, so I figured I should just get to asking questions.

"Willie, how did you get hurt? Was it those same schoolkids from the fair?" I said, a ghost of menace in my voice. I knew forgiveness was the right thing in every situation, but right then I just wanted to teach those kids a lesson.

He nodded and stared off into the fire. Then he began to speak. "I was just headed back here from... from where I been. And they came outta nowhere. Yellin' nasty things, shoutin', they circled 'round me and got to throwin' stuff. Dirt, sticks, anythin' they could find. Then one of'em got it into his head to throw somethin' a little bit bigger, and soon enough they was all throwin' stones and rocks. I managed to block most of'em, until the head o' their pack grabbed a right ol' boulder and chucked it at my head. Blood started gushin', and made the ground dark red. When they saw I was bleedin' so bad, they took off runnin'. Right off, I started for here. But I got dizzier and dizzier as I went, and I don't a'member much past that." He shrugged, dark circles under his eyes. I peered at him carefully, accepting the story. Then I remembered something.

"Right afore you passed out, Willie, you told me a little bit about what happened to you," I said slowly. "You said something   curious."

Right away, alarm flashed all over his face. He struggled to hide it, but Willie'd never been good at keeping his feelings off his face, and I'd only gotten to know him even better recently. There was no way this would end without me knowing more.

"You told me that those kids were yelling 'orphan' at you," I declared, watching his face. Willie swallowed and his cheeks flushed dark in the shadows. The leaping fire cast strange light on the two of us, thin, dancing coils of darkness and shade. His eyes glittered with some emotion I couldn't quite identify. It looked like a mixture of terrible anxiety, alarm, fear, and... relief.

After watching the battling feelings on his face for quite some time, I shook his shoulder. "Willie, just tell me what's going on. Can't you trust us?"

He hesitated, and then dropped his head. I could barely make out what he was saying then, 'cause he started to mumble. "...didn't tell no one when it happened, 'cause back then, I were all alone. I didn't have no one to talk to, no one to trust. Now I got you all, but... I was afeared that you'd not want me hangin' about no more. And asides, the right time to go tellin' you all never came up. Since I got left behind, I been eatin' when I could. What was left 'round our home, of the crops. My pops taught me a right long time ago how t'live in the woods, what t'eat and what not t'eat. So I been okay. But in the night, when it's dark and I'm alone, I a'member how twisted up he was when he died, I a'member the way the candles had burnt out..." He trailed off. When he finally looked up at me, I could see the tears streaming down his face, glistening in the firelight.

I sighed heavily. "Willie, what happened? Why were you alone? When did all this living off the land stuff start?" A torn, twitching smile grew on his face, and combined with his tears, his expression struck chords inside me. I knew that look. I knew what somebody looked like when they were trying not to cry, when they were smiling a broken smile so they wouldn't break down weeping. It was the look I'd seen on Papa's face after Mama went away. It was the look that plagued my mind, the look that said, *"You're never going to be whole again."* The look I saw in the mirror whenever I thought too hard about Mama. Willie looked right at me with that broken smile and those streaming tears.

"I never had a ma," He said softly. "I mean, she died when I was born. She died wakin' me up into the world." I just shook my head, choked up with the realization that Willie and I were more alike than I'd ever known.

"But this... this all started when I came home from town one day, and I found Pa lyin' in bed, all cold and still-like. He... he looked at me, an' he said, 'Vivian? That you?' And I said, 'No, Pa. It's me, Willie. Your boy.' But Pa just looked past me and said, 'Vivian. Time for me t'go home.' And he held out his arms, and th' light in his eyes went out, and he jus' sorta crumpled down, still as anythin'. I shook him and shook him and started to cry and scream but he wouldn't wake up." Willie's breath was whispery and ragged, like it was fading in and out of him without a will.

"Then I noticed everythin' 'round him. There was cloth, all bloody, and a knife. Pa... his leg..." Willie got real quiet. His voice fell softly in the shadowy air, like tiny droplets of rain pattering the ground, nearly inaudible.

"Pa's leg was swelled up all awful-like. He went and tied a cloth 'round it real tight, right above the swellin'. And it was cut open. He musta got bit by a rattler and gone home to try an' patch hisself up, suck out the poison." Willie trembled. "Pa did always think he could fix everythin' on his own." Willie paused, eyes shut tight. I looked on silently, worried but not willing to speak in case my words failed me.

Willie took a breath and continued. "Nobody came for me, and I didn't go lookin' for nobody. I took care o' things, and tried not to think about... about bein' an orphan." He looked at me, head tilted to one side.

"But at night, when I was alone, everythin' I'd said wrong to my Pa came back at me. I won't never forget. Can't forget." His voice broke. Then he put his small hands up to his face and cried and cried. He coughed and sobbed out, his weeping striking at my heart with icy talons. I hugged my knees and just sat with Willie.

Sat with him while he cried.

CHAPTER NINE

Willie fell back asleep that night, after he had nothing left inside him. I slept too, on my sheets in the kitchen. The next morning I woke before anyone else, as if my mind were on a timer. I felt dulled by exhaustion, but I tried to busy myself with breakfast, not willing to dwell on everything that was happening to us. The crops were in danger, as dust had begun to roll in with a vengeance. Lily was wasting away in a shadowy room, and I now understood about Willie. Why he always, and I do mean *always*, had permission to come over for supper. Why he'd never taken us to his home – He had no home, not anymore! – Why his folks never needed him to work.

The bright, sunny morning where I'd first met Willie popped into my head, and I recalled wondering if his parents didn't come to church. I remembered thinking that absurd, and just assuming he had a sick sibling or some other home emergency. Now it all made terrible, ice-cold sense. Willie didn't have any parents. He didn't have a home. I was fiercely grateful then, that we'd accepted him so. Then I winced. Those kids hadn't been exactly accepting of Willie. First they'd got on him because of his hair color and the way he looked, and then 'cause he was an orphan.

Orphan. It was such an ugly word to describe somebody who'd lost their mama and their papa. Bitter amazement always slid into my heart when I thought about it. Willie's parents were dead, so the monsters threw rocks at him? I shivered with rage. Humanity was becoming something awful, something darker than we were meant to be. Sometimes kids were the absolute cruelest. I stopped mulling over the injustice of it all for a moment and wondered how exactly they'd found out about Willie's parents. Where had he gone? Where could he have possibly gone that those kids had found out so easily about his terrible situation? I heard someone enter the kitchen and looked up. Papa was there, face tired and worried.

"How's Willie?" He asked. The night before, I hadn't explained much to him. Just told him what Willie had said, and asked him to carry Willie to the couch. He'd complied, helped me clean and tend to the wound, and then ordered me to rest before retiring himself. I sighed and prepared myself to explain everything.

"Papa, Willie's alright now. You were right about it just being a shallow cut, and he woke just fine in the middle of the night. We got to talking about what happened." I paused, thinking over my words. Papa looked at me with narrowed gray eyes, clearly sensing my weighty explanation. "Papa, you know how Willie's never asked us to his home, or met us to his parents?" I said.

"Yes," Papa nodded. "and...?"

"I'm gettin' there!" I bristled. Then I sagged against the cupboards and took a deep breath. "Papa, Willie's Mama died a real long time ago when he was born. And more recently, his Papa died from a rattler."

Papa's shoulders sagged and he put one hand on his face and sighed, real slow and sad-like. Then he swallowed very hard and rubbed at his throat with a tired hand. "Feared as much." He said thickly. "I had only hoped it weren't true. I planned on askin' 'round 'bout the boy, but I just never got to it, what with all that's been goin' on."

Papa's face took on a look of realization. "So it were Willie, then," he said, looking relieved. "That's all."

"What?" I asked, confused.

Papa shook himself and ran a hand through his graying hair as he explained. "I been findin' some things in the barn that seem t'point to somebody livin' there," he said. "Like somebody been sleepin' in there in the deep o' night and vanishin' before the mornin' comes. Musta been Willie. But how'd he make it afore he came t' be with us?"

My eyebrows rose in bewilderment and I shook my head slightly as I answered him. "Apparently, Willie knows lots about the forests and such. He's just been surviving off what he can find as far as food goes." Papa's face betrayed a pained expression. He rubbed his eyelids and swallowed again.

I shook my head; the corners of my lips twitched up into a regretful crescent shape, and I spoke quietly. "That nasty group of school kids from the fair, the ones I told you about? Well, they followed him to wherever he went yesterday, and when he got back to the fork they circled around and ambushed him, throwing rocks and all manner of horrid things. When they hurt him real bad, y'know, that cut on his head, they ran off, cowards. And he stumbled home and that was that." I shrugged helplessly.

Papa nodded, his expression darkening. "Somethin' will have to be done about them," He said coldly, pure disappointment clear in his storming eyes. Then, resolved over that, he cleared his throat and managed a feeble smile. "Well," he said, trying to sound bright, "ain't stuff just worked out? God clearly got a plan for this boy." And this sparked a real smile from me.

"Yeah, Papa, sure enough. I've been so proud of Lily and you, honestly. Once he told me what happened, I just couldn't stop thinking about where he'd be if he hadn't fallen into things around our home. This is all because I met him in the church that Sunday." I paused. "All because God brought him there, to shake hands with me, all odd and whatnot, side to side," I said softly. I smiled again, at the memory, and then Willie padded into the room unsteadily.

He offered a weak grin to Papa, saying, "Sorry I been so much trouble, sir. I woulda told y'sooner, truth, but I didn't know rightly how."

"Oh, get off it, boy! I couldn't be more forgivin' if you was my own kin." Papa pulled him into a bear hug, patting his head around the bandages. Willie broke out laughing, and Papa let him go, and soon enough we were all feeling much better. A good cry and a good laugh are all you need sometimes, to heal the wounds caused by the deepest secrets. Willie's sadness at his Papa's loss would belong with him always, just like I always thought about Mama, but he could start to breathe easy again about his life. 'Cause here he was with us, and no way were we sending him out into them dumb forests to live alone. Here he belonged, and here he'd stay. With us. Lily always did miss her Bubba when he left, anyhow. Now she'd never have to miss him again.

CHAPTER TEN

Papa tried to adopt Willie all legal-like, but the town's official didn't seem to care a bit. He'd said, "*If* the boy's an orphan, he'll be shipped to the city orphanage." He'd said it like Willie was an item to be tossed about freely.

Papa had looked at the man like he was crazy. "I just told ya he's an orphan. But he don't wanna go to the city, we wanna have him stay with us. Permanent, like." He had said, real firmly.

The man had looked at Papa meaningfully. "I never heard that. I said... *if* he's an orphan, he'll be shipped to the city. That's all there is to it. If he *has* a father," He'd said pointedly, looking over the tops of his spectacles at my Papa, "then there's no need to take action, is there?" Then he'd closed-up shop, gone home, skedaddled. And Papa seemed to get the message. Nobody cared if we took in an orphan who had nowhere to go. If we didn't tell, nobody else would.

Right after we tried to adopt Willie, I decided I could ask him a question that'd been growing in my mind since the night he was injured. I turned to him one day while we were washing dishes.

"Willie, I've got a question for you," I said, hesitating, "since you're with us now and everything."

Willie blinked at me. "Yeah?" he said as he scrubbed at a pot that had been used for stew.

"Well, I know it's personal, and you were really protective of all this before," I said slowly, "but since we know the truth now, I was wondering..." I trailed off, hoping I wasn't being insensitive. Willie just kept scrubbing, glancing at me. "I was wondering where you went that day, when you were injured," I said softly. "Where did you go that was so important, and so secret and all? And how'd those kids know you were an orphan?" Willie flinched at the word, and I felt guilt gnaw on me. "How did they know your pa and ma went away?" I said again, softer this time.

Willie hesitated and put the pot down next to the tub of soapy water, wiping his hands on his trousers. Then he looked up at me, his bright eyes vacant. "After Pa died, I buried 'im. Next to Ma. There were a real lonely place a few miles down th' way from us, in a valley full o' wildflowers." He gazed out the window, his eyes empty, his consciousness lost in his memories.

"That's where Ma was buried," he said, completely still. "I planted some o' them yellow flowers on her grave, and the blue ones on Pa's. Those was their favorites colors." He stared outside for a few moments.

I hated to disturb him, but I was still curious. "So those kids followed you to the graves and realized you were alone?" I asked quietly.

Willie nodded. Then he turned to look into my eyes, his own lined with tears. "That's why it were real important for me t' visit 'em," he said desperately. "I went to tell 'em about you all. My new family," he said proudly. "I went to tell 'em about my lil sister who was sick and to ask them to maybe pray for her. And to tell 'em about you and your fancy talkin', and my new Pa, and how he been so kind and all. Ma n' Pa was my family once, but I was pretty sure I'd found myself a new one. So I had to say goodbye."

I choked back feelings and the tears in my throat and said, "They'd be happy for you, Willie. They would."

After that, I didn't ask any more questions, and Willie came to live with us permanently. We set him up a little area in the front room. The couch became his bed at night and went back to being our couch in the day. He washed up at night in the kitchen. Things were just fine.

One day, quick like a flash, everything changed. I was out with Willie, feeding the chickens. We'd already gotten most of our chores done, now we just had to finish things up. The few cattle we had left were out grazing and the chickens were out of their coop, in the chicken-yard, pecking up seed that we threw for 'em. Willie ran out and off toward the barn to fetch more.

The dust storm hit like lightning and left ruins in its wake.

One moment I was watching Willie disappear into the barn, the huge red door swinging shut behind him, and the next I was feeling like a weed in the wind. All I felt was dust. In my mouth, my ears, clawing at my wrenched-shut eyelids, driving against my skin like a million tiny sharp mosquitos. I gasped and inhaled dust, coughing and coughing. A vicious cycle began. Coughing, inhaling, coughing. All the while I was being smothered by the dark cloud of dust and its wind.

Eventually I hit the ground and stayed down, lying on my stomach. I wrenched my shirt up and fixed it over my mouth, trying desperately to find clean air to breath. It helped a little bit, and I cleared out my clotted lungs best I could. I could barely see anything, could hardly open my eyes, couldn't hear. Just a rushing, muffled sound of whirling dust. I fought back to my feet with my shirt over my mouth. Fighting the wind, dirty tears streaming, I took step after chaotic step. Out of nowhere, a post of wood flew into my view and hit me in the head, hard. I staggered back.

Suddenly my hands and arms tingled. I looked at them in wonder, flexing them as much as I could. The dust had slackened a bit; I could see in front of me. I coughed against the dust. Water was pouring over me now, it must be raining! I felt elation rush through me. I touched the water flowing down my head and looked at my hand... I stared in confusion at the dark blood dripping from my fingers. My ears were ringing. Sudden exhaustion swept over me, a heaviness stronger than iron, and I gave in to the torrent of dust and darkness.

Pain.

My first conscious thought was an acknowledgment of the stinging pain all over, inside, outside. I felt like I'd taken a bath in sharp rocks, and swallowed half the water. I could feel blood on my skin. My lungs burned and my eyes throbbed in their sockets. My back ached. Very slowly I tried to sit up, only succeeding in causing a fresh wave of powerful, dizzying darkness to sweep over my eyes.

So I lay back down, desperately trying to think of anything to do to help myself. I took shuddering breaths, my lungs burning like fire and my entire body itching with a dire intensity. There was nothing but dust above me, hanging in the air like an ominous storm cloud. I gave up and lay still, staring up. Then I began to shiver, even though my skin was radiating heat. My skin felt as though it was worn thin like the pages of my bible, and I choked as incomprehensible pain stifled all my breath. Suddenly a buzzing numbness crawled over my face and spread slowly down my neck, soothing the pain that had been twitching over my flesh. I sighed in relief and tried to sit when the numbness slid over me completely and the pain vanished. But my arms turned to liquid half-way up, a wave of darkness and nausea swept over me... and I slept.

Willie waited for his eyes to adjust in the dark interior of the barn. Several shafts of sunlight pervaded its solid roof, and one glanced over Willie's startling red hair without discrimination. His eyes had just fallen upon the great sack of feed in the corner when he became aware of a loud rushing sound. He turned around, wariness bright in his liquid eyes. Golden, dancing light shone through the slightly open barn door. He marveled at the dust motes that swirled and spun in eddies of the light. Suddenly the barn door slammed shut, the wind howling against it, and the storm truly began.

The rushing grew louder, and dust began to creep inside the barn. It filtered in like poison seeping through a vein, at first slowly and carefully. Then it began to tear at the barn like a vengeful giant long scorned. The door of the barn was straining, bowing inward under the weight of dust piling against it. Willie darted his eyes around in alarm, every muscle tensed. All he could imagine was the barn's roof being swept away and the storm plucking him out easy as a fish from a stream. He turned frantically about, searching for anything to protect himself with.

As the light streaming through the roof began to die, he saw in its quickly failing embrace a pile of empty potato sacks and a bucket full of water. Willie ran over and lifted the large bucket. Water spilled out and soaked the rough fibers of the sacks; when they were thoroughly doused, Willie dropped the bucket and peeled back some of the sacks. He crawled underneath them and lay shivering in their wet arms, pressing his mouth against the rough material. He breathed filtered air as the sunlight died completely and left the barn a swirling void of dust as black as pitch.

Willie waited in the darkness, his eyes strongly shut. He felt himself shivering as dust stroked at the sides of his arms and legs, which were exposed. It threaded about him, and the rushing noise was everything in that chasm of darkness, a loud, echoing waterfall of dust, a deluge of soil, raining from the sky and reaching for him through the blackness. He did not know how long it went on, only that it ended as quickly as it had come.

He was aware of nothing at first, and then he registered the silence. No rushing, no thundering whisper of dust swirling about him. He cautiously pulled aside the heavy sacks, and then pushed them off him in relief. The air was still around him, though completely saturated in dust. He blinked and coughed as wheezing seized his chest; Willie's eyes began to water as his body tried to rid itself of the foreign invader inside it. Willie coughed, and then drew in a rasping breath, steadying himself. His throat was raw and sore. He scrubbed at the skin along his arms and legs and tried to focus.

Suddenly, adrenaline rushed through him like lightning. His heart squeezed painfully, energy coursing through him and pulling the ache away from him, for now. He drew in a sick breath as he realized with desperation that Alex must have been out in the dust.

Willie ran and stumbled to the far side of the barn, and his raw fingers pushed against the barn door, and he wailed in frustration as it wouldn't open. He gritted his teeth and threw himself upon the door, hating how little he weighed, hating the monstrous obstacle in front of him. In his mind, a picture of pounds of dust piled against the great heavy timbers mocked him, and he gritted his teeth, knowing he'd have to find some other way out.

He whirled around, searching. The dust had slammed the doors shut, meaning it'd come from the east. He ran to the west side of the barn, remembering the hole in the wall where the cats came through.

He could see outside.

Willie grabbed a shovel and began to rip at the wood, enlarging the hole as much as he could. Chips of wood flew through the air, and then he was done, and he was crawling out, the ragged wood pulling at his hair, and then he was standing upright, outside, free.

"Alex…! Alex!" He choked and fell to the ground on his hands and knees, wrestling for breath in the dust-infected air.

As soon as he caught his second wind, he stood painfully and took staggering steps outward, toward where he thought

Alex had been. He squinted through the sunny haze of tinted air, and down the road, he saw a crumpled mass beside the fence. Stabbing pain with sharp, hooked claws grabbed his heart as he recognized Alex and more energy pumped through him. Willie ran.

He fell to his knees beside her, bile and dread rising in his throat. She was balled up loosely into a curled mass on the ground, and her skin was dirty. Willie leaned over her and his lungs wouldn't draw breath when he saw the amount of blood flowing from her skull. It was spread under her, staining the soil with dark crimson. Willie shivered with terror as he leaned close to her mouth, listening for breath... silence greeted him. Horror grew in his throat, pulling at his lips as they twitched and danced in agony. His friend, his best friend... dead?

Willie shut his eyes and shook his head, tears clawing at his face, terrible, warm molasses rising behind his nose and eyes. He felt his limbs go numb. A choking sound escaped him. Willie crumpled to the ground next to Alex, his eyes staring sightlessly at the sky. He breathed shallowly, hardly, not caring. Not caring.

Everything was lost.

The horrible, twitching expression of loss grew on his face as he fought back sobs of rage and grief. The Lord didn't love him. He hated Willie. He'd taken his Pa and his Ma, and now Willie's friend. His best friend. Willie curled loosely in a ball, eyes shut tight in fury and helplessness, crying out in great aching torment. Everything was lost.

Alex shivered next to him.

At first, Willie dismissed the movement. It didn't even register inside him that his friend – his *dead* friend – just moved. Then she shivered again and cried out in her unconsciousness, and Willie froze in shock. Warmth flooded through him, then strength, and he took a breath as night turned to day. Willie turned to her, jittery with hope, and tried to lift her. He groaned – Alex was heavy! He left off trying to carry her and stood from his kneeling position. He turned back to the barn, moving as fast as his limbs would take him.

Suddenly there was a searing pain in his chest, like tiny knives in his heart. Willie gasped and fell to the ground, choking for air. He rubbed at his chest with one hand, trying to breathe. Willie gulped hard, and the pain inside him faded to a dull ache. He got to his feet, wheezing, and turned once again to the barn. Panic had set in slowly, like a cautious ghost, crawling inside him and trying to commandeer his mind. He shook off the tendrils of alarm and ran around to the cat hole. Then he was inside again, grabbing at a large potato sack, crawling back out, running.

Willie laid the sack out next to Alex, and then tried to lift her onto it. He half carried, half rolled her on. Then he grabbed onto it and began to drag his precious burden home. The blood on Alex, mixed with dust and dirt, smeared on the sack as they travelled. Willie sensed heat leaving her, her skin cooling quickly. She whimpered as her arm brushed against the fence bordering the road, and Willie swerved away from it. He didn't want her to hurt. He murmured apologies as he rushed them over the dusty ground. Her life depended on his ability to get her home.

Tear-stains streaked Alex's face, trailed through her dirty and smudged skin. Willie glanced down at her and an ache rose inside him. He couldn't forget the despair he'd felt, faced with her supposed death. To lose her was not an option. How could he face Papa and Lily if Alex was gone? He would have to find a new home. They wouldn't want him anymore.

He bit his lip angrily as he realized the way his thoughts were heading. It wasn't that he didn't want her to die because he wanted a home. He didn't want her to die... couldn't let Alex die because she was his best friend. To prove to himself that he cared about Alex, he decided he would leave once she was better. To prove that he wasn't using them for a home.

Willie steeled himself and lifted Alex through the doorway. He staggered and strained against her weight. Willie leaned against the counter, using it to lever himself and keep his hold on Alex. He stood just inside the kitchen, wondering what to do. He could feel the life seeping out of her body as he stood there dumbly. Then, suddenly, Papa was there. He skidded into the room, gasping, and fell against the wall, trying to catch his breath.

"Came... from town... soon as... the storm... quit..." He choked out.

Papa caught sight of Alex then, bleeding in Willie's arms. He stood upright and all the color drained from his face... then iron filled his eyes. He would not let his daughter die. He took her silently from Willie, not bothering to say a word to the boy. Papa crossed into the front room and laid her carefully on the couch. She shuddered softly as the material touched her wounded skin. Papa turned to Willie, his cold gray eyes empty of emotion.

"Fetch a basin of water. Bring any clean cloth we have."

Willie scrambled to obey, even as he felt the energy fading from his body. He was worn and tired, but he shoved down the empty feeling of exhaustion and kept moving, knowing Alex's life was on the line. He couldn't sleep yet. Willie gathered the things Papa would need and dropped them in a bundle next to the sofa. He had fetched clean water. He stood silently by, waiting.

Papa anxiously soaked a cloth in the water and began to carefully dab at Alex's wounds. Her blood was mixed with the dust and drying in a disgusting coat of mud over her sand-papered skin. Papa took a look at her head. Dark red blood had matted her sandy hair to her scalp – it was still running from the crack in her head. He shaved away part of her hair to get to the injury easier. Willie was running back and forth the whole time, exchanging rusty-red tinted water for clean. Papa washed away the blood and mud, and then took a look at the wound. He shook his head helplessly. "It'll need stitches." So Willie ran to fetch the stitchin' kit from the barn.

Papa took a deep breath and set in one roughshod stitch to keep the wound shut. He began to bind her head in clean cloth, tying the ends loosely to keep them from slipping off. After he'd finished cleaning away the blood, Papa surveyed his work with dark worry in his eyes. Her head was mostly swathed in cloth. She breathed shallowly, fighting demons of pain even in her sleep. Willie bit his lip and looked away. Papa pointed to the floor.

"Stay here. You can sleep if y'gotta, but stay near Alex. She might be needin' you if she wakes."

Willie, his brain blurred with exhaustion, wondered aloud, "Where you going to, sir?"

Papa looked down at his daughter with icy fear on his face. "To fetch the Doc. I ain't got nothin' here to clean 'er head properly afore stitchin' it up completely. Doc'll have to come. We ain't got no time to dally 'round. Otherfolk'll be up there soon too, needin' help." Papa shook his head. "I hope she ain't breathed in much o' that dust, but aside from that her head's gonna need lookin' at. Could be messed up on the inside, and infection's real likely."

Willie nodded – he knew they'd covered her wound not because it was severe but because even a smaller injury could put one's life at risk. Infection would be an enemy now. Then Papa vanished out the door, and Willie fell against the side of the sofa and sank into fitful rest, spurred into sleep only by utter exhaustion. His dreams were shallow and filled with Alex's death, her flesh crawling over him and whispering through bloody teeth, *"Your fault. Your fault..."*

CHAPTER ELEVEN

I was floating.

My mind forgot the world – forgot Lily, forgot myself, Alex, forgot Papa – I even forgot Mama. For but a moment that lasted a lifetime, I floated in the recesses of dark peace. Nothing plagued my conscience; no guilt, no anger, no regret. Every responsibility, every need was gone. I felt no pain; I felt nothing but the thick darkness around me. I was simply floating. I tried to move my hands and giggled, because they were tingling. The echoing shadows around me threw my giggles back at me, again and again. It was a crescendo of airy sound. I listened in fascination, feeling childish with awe. What was this place?

I could see now. The darkness was all around me, but if I stared far enough into it, things took shape. Translucent, beautiful things that called to me. I swam toward them, my fingers parting the darkness with a rain of falling glass shadows.

Time seemed against me, and the closer I got to the swimming jellyfish-type objects, the more they seemed to stretch and twist away without ever actually moving. A current of cold cut through the dark and caught me, spinning me further from my goal. I felt my mind drifting as the ice numbed my thoughts; I wanted to give in, to drift with the breeze, to forget. But something heavy and insistent inside me demanded that I fight – demanded that I *remember*. There was a warmth beckoning me, a current that I knew would help me fight. So I sighed and opened back up to the darkness, awoke myself, my mind sharpening with the effort. I struggled toward my destination, feeling more determined with every stroke of my arms against the shadow-air. Finally I could see the objects with closer detail; they could in fact be reached.

I swam up closer to one of them, the object still tantalizingly out of my reach. It was pulsing softly, slivers of light dancing through it in a beautiful pattern. The thing had clear skin with swirling strokes of silver inside it; the object was lovely, yet it was not alive. This I knew.

With everything inside me, I strained to reach out and touch it. I did not know in this moment what would happen when I did, and yet I knew deep inside me somewhere that it was essential. That it was part of my waking up. I knew that this moment was where I fought for my life – that this decided my fate.

So I fought.

As the darkness around me contorted and bent to swallow me up, I stretched out to touch the object... I gasped and stiffened as a rush of pain shot through me. Memories, anguish, all of it much more real than this dark world of forgetfulness, melted from the recesses of my frozen mind. She came back to me in a bolt of agony – Mama, my mama... How could I forget? How could I ever forget?

The weight that had been lifted from me descended once again onto my shoulders, and I remembered something else... that in a dream of a dream, from long ago, my head was hurting...

Alex thrashed in her sleep, crying out as her wounds sent pain shooting through her. Willie was awake and standing next to the couch, eyes shadowed and hooded with worry. He got a cool cloth and placed it on Alex's head, murmuring to steady his own nerves. He felt like his heart was shaking, fearful for his friend's life. Her inane mumblings made no sense to him, but every now and again he caught the word *Mama*. Every time, he felt intense sorrow for his friend, who'd lost the one she loved most dearly and still fought for life, fought to care for the ones Mama had left behind.

Willie wandered to the door and looked out, waiting. Papa had to be back soon, with the doctor. He glanced over at the back of Alex's head and drew in a sharp breath; her bandages were turning red from the inside out. He looked away, nausea rising inside him. Alex was a fighter. There was a reason she always won at arm wrestling. Willie smiled to himself. He had to believe that Alex would be okay, that all of his efforts had not been in vain. She was his family now. Lily needed her, Papa needed her, *Willie* needed her... The night may be dark for now, but surely the dawn would come soon.

Willie straightened and put a hand to his eyes, squinting out into the evening light. Was that Papa running down the path, with the doctor in tow? But everything inside him wilted and died as he realized that Papa was alone.

Running and alone.

The combination didn't make sense, couldn't mean anything good. He refused to think about it. Willie just stood and waited for Papa to reach him. He waited and choked every thought that tried to draw breath inside him. He would not betray Alex with his mind, not here, not now, when he didn't know anything. He would not think.

Papa jogged up to the threshold, his face grim. Something was tucked under his arm. Shadows lay over the path outside in excess, proof of the descending night. The long night that was yet to come. Willie looked at Papa with his unspoken question. What would they do now for Alex? Papa drew his bundle out from his grip and set it down on the kitchen table. He turned to Willie with apologies in his eyes.

"Soon as I got to the Doc's, he were already gone. The nurse sent me t'the general store an' told me to ask for this, said it were far better than any animal kits folk keep 'round." Willie looked at the bundle beside Papa, trying to understand. It was a medical kit, of course, but what had the nurse meant when she said the contents were better'n that of an animal kit? Papa unwrapped it and Willie's eyes fell on the things that rolled out. A square brown bottle of liquid, bandages, cloth, a sewing needle, and strong-looking white thread. There was a little tube of paste, too, something labeled *Miracle Heal*. Willie shook his head, fear in his eyes. Would this tiny kit be enough to save his best friend?

Papa set his teeth at the necessary task before him. "I'm gonna clean her head wound 'n then I'll stitch it right up, proper this time." He spoke aloud, sort of to Willie, sort of to himself, as if he were convincing them both it wouldn't be so bad. Papa hesitated then, fingers hovering over the supplies. Willie nodded at him, and for a brief moment, weakness and uncertainty showed in Papa's eyes. Then they were all steel again.

Papa picked up the brown bottle, the cloth, and the thread. Willie grabbed the needle as they headed for the couch. Willie sat near Alex with the needle in his trembling fingers, waiting. Papa sat down on a stool in front of Alex. She was lying on the couch, her head propped up. Papa unwrapped the blood-soiled cloth around her head, examining the shaved patch. He poured liquid from the brown bottle on some cloth and then washed Alex's wound gently but firmly. It must have stung, but Papa clearly knew that pain now could mean no infection later. Alex muttered in her unconsciousness, trying to roll over and away from Papa's burning treatment.

Willie kept her still and said softly, "Don't worry, Alex. We'll always be here waitin' for you." Tears beaded in his eyes as he spoke; the words only built pain inside him. Papa had tossed aside the used cloth. He poured liquid from the brown bottle over the needle and then threaded it.

Willie swallowed and took two steps back. "Sir, I don't rightly think I be able t'watch this."

Papa's steeled gaze fell on Willie and then softened when they saw his fear. "Y'don't gotta watch, Willie. Ain't nothin' you gotta see." Willie nodded, terror stealing his voice, and turned away. He felt slightly ashamed, as though he should be watching like a man.

'But you're just a boy,' said Alex's voice in his mind. He knew she would say something like that, if she could read his thoughts. Willie glanced back at her. If she were awake... He shook himself and looked away. Papa had moved his hands over Alex's skull now. Willie knew he couldn't bear to see this part. Alex cried out for a moment and then sank into deeper unconsciousness, her movements stilling. Papa cut off his emotions and completed his grueling work – sewing shut his daughter's wound. Papa washed the finished suture, smearing it with *Miracle Heal,* and then bandaged it firmly.

"Infection'd find it right difficult t'get in there," Papa said with a weak attempt at a smile.

Willie turned and looked. His stomach flipped with relief when he realized it was over and done with – he wouldn't have to look at the awful wound anymore.

Time crawled by slowly, taunting Papa and Willie with its agonizing tread. Seconds seemed to turn to hours, to days, to years. Every moment stretched out endlessly with Alex shallowly breathing before the two; a father staring down on his hurting child, and a young brother with fear mocking his every thought. Finally, fate took pity on them; Alex fell asleep quietly. She seemed peaceful enough. Now that her injury was covered and taken care of, the awful, dire feeling of the situation slipped away. Willie slid to the ground, dizzy with relief and exhaustion.

Papa glanced down at him and said, "Careful, son! I can't be fixin' up two o'my kids, y'hear?"

Willie felt warmth flush through him when Papa called him *one o' his kids*. Willie hadn't been called that in so long. The ache inside him felt soothed at this; he had a home here, one he never had to leave. One where he never had to prove himself or be anyone else, or be good enough, or feel unloved. Willie *was* home here.

And it felt just right.

CHAPTER TWELVE

I had no idea where I was when I awoke. The couch I was laying on, the pale painted walls around me, the ugly old rug on the floor before me – it took a moment for the familiarity of my surroundings to set in.

I sat upright to look around, but before I got very far, sharp pain jittered over me. I felt it in my skin, on my face – and in a dull throb in the back of my head. I tensed up in pain. Suddenly, a sharp, unbearable tickling began in my lungs. I coughed once, a harsh, raspy sound that made my ears shiver, and a horrible pain hammered my head. I stopped instantly, whimpering, my chest heaving as I tried to hold in the coughing. Eventually the tickling faded to a dull itch, and I recalled all that had occurred.

Everything came back to me in a flash – someone had to have found me outside after the storm and carried me back here. I wondered who it'd been.

"Alex! You're awake!" Came a cheerful voice behind me. I turned my sore neck to see Willie's beaming face. He looked so incredibly happy to see me. I smiled weakly at him.

"How long was I out, Willie?" I knew I'd been unconscious, for vague memories of strange dreams were floating about inside my head. Something about fighting, about remembering. I couldn't quite recall.

Willie shook his head slowly. "After I found ya outside, all bleedin' on the ground, I dragged you back here an' you was passed out through allat. Then yer Pa stitched y'up and cleaned your wounds and such. After that, you slept for two days. I was worried right well, but Pa was twice as calm. He said, 'Give 'er time, Willard. She'll waken soon as the bacon's on the table!'"

I laughed weakly with Willie, but I watched his face closer than anything. I wanted to know how bad things had actually been. Papa's jokes were often his way of dealing with tough times. Willie looked at me and made a secretive face, speaking in a loud whisper.

"'Course, your Pa's too cheap to even buy you some purty flowers!" I shook my head in mock horror, laughter fluttering softly inside me. I was still so tired. My face went completely blank when I saw Papa come in and stand behind Willie. I looked at him with wide eyes, wondering what he'd heard. Willie's smile slowly dropped until he was frowning.

"What are y'lookin' at?" He went to turn, but Papa roared and put him in a headlock.

"Imagine.. Th' nerve..." Papa grunted. "This'un calls me cheap?" He sniffed. "Hurts m'feelings."

I couldn't help laughing at the silliness of it all. Papa and Willie wrestled for a moment or two, grunting and squealing like pigs as they tormented one another. Then Papa pushed Willie over and danced over to me. Willie flailed on the ground for a moment and then gave up, his clothes dusty and ruffled. He lay on the ground and pretended to be a slab of bacon, yelling, "Eat me!" with his arms and legs stuck straight up. I loved bacon.

I was laughing so hard now that I was coughing and finding it hard to breathe. My head was throbbing, but the laughter felt good on my heart.

Papa sat down across me and waited for me to catch my breath, his smile wide. "So, how y'doin'?" He asked, making a ridiculously over-concerned face.

I took a slow breath. "Quit makin' me laugh, you pair of saps. My skull aches to high heaven an' I can't breathe!"

Papa nodded understandingly.

Willie had been creeping up behind Papa. He stopped and grinned briefly at me, waving. Then he continued stalking, his tongue stuck out in concentration. I let out a snort of laughter, and Papa followed my gaze, catching Willie mid-creep. He gasped, and then bowled Willie over playfully with a sweep of his arm. Willie went down and stayed down, curled on the floor.

I looked over at him, suddenly and irrationally concerned. His face was pinched with pain and one hand was over his heart.

I glanced at Papa and then reached out to tap Willie on the shoulder. "Willie, are you okay?" He glanced up at me, pain evident in his face, and then it vanished.

He bounced up off the ground and then down the hallway, calling over his shoulder, "Somebody wants t'see you!" I just sat there shaking my head.

A slow dragging sound came from down the hallway. I looked on with heavy eyes, heart laden with apprehension yet hopeful all at once. Lily came limping down the hall. She leaned heavily on Willie as she dragged her twisted knee along. There was so much exhaustion on her face, so much effort creasing her forehead. My breath felt thick inside me. As she neared the couch, she broke away from Willie and stumbled, her feet twisting and trying to keep balance. She fell against the couch, and I caught her.

"Lil!" I cried. "You're out of bed!"

She looked up at me, her face flushed with color for once. "I wanted to see Oxie and make sure she was better," She explained calmly with a flash of her old self. I looked incredulously at Willie, who was next to her.

He shrugged, grinning. "She wanted t'see you. It were her idea."

"That's amazing, really amazing, Lily. Thanks for comin' to see me, even though I'm not that badly injured." The words tumbled out of me.

Willie raised an eyebrow. "Oh, you ain't?" He said knowingly. What did he know that I didn't? I hated it when people knew things that I didn't.

"Not at all," I declared. "Stop looking at me like you know something!"

He just nodded at me and said, "Try t'get up, then."

I looked at him like this was ridiculous, and then I stood. Murky darkness swept over me and consumed my thoughts, and I sank involuntarily back down onto the sofa. Well, darn.

I touched my head hesitantly and then glowered at Willie. "How did you know I'd be dizzy?"

He rolled his eyes. "Stands t'reason, Alex. Y'got hit in the head by somethin' big and heavy. I'd be goin' pretty dizzy if'n that ever happened t'me."

I mimicked his words with annoyance as he spoke, and then my gaze snapped to Lily as she began to speak.

"Alex, please don't hurt yourself," She begged, coughing. I felt my heart pinch in anger that she could stand there and worry about me while her own limbs fought against her every day. I tugged her ponytail lightly.

"I promise I'll get better, Lil," I said absently. I was wondering now if *Lily* was ever going to get better, to be anything more than a worn-out doll, feeling discarded and forgotten. My own health was the last thing on my mind. It was the least important, anyhow.

Lily took my hand happily, smiling her little gap-toothed grin. "Good, Oxie! I don't wanna say goodbye." She said. Papa looked at her, rigid with shock.

"What did you say?" Asked Willie slowly.

Lily glanced at him with her brown eyes, saying, "I don't wanna say goodbye yet. Mama had to leave so quick. I want Alex to stay."

My eyes fogged over as I stared, forgetting to blink. It... hurt. Her words hurt me, bittersweet and sickening. How could she just say something like that? Lily grimaced and one of her hands went to her knee. Willie looked at her and tapped her lightly on the shoulder.

"I think it's time to rest, Lil Monster," He said.

Watching Lily painstakingly make her way back to the bedroom, I felt a mixture of emotions well up inside me. White-hot anger bubbled frothily against an ice-cold block of sadness that I had been carrying inside for a while. My thoughts burned with resentment and fear, regret and sorrow. It wasn't fair. It wasn't fair.

"Alex, y'need anythin'? You ain't got nothin' to eat in two days," said Papa. I shook myself and looked up at him.

"What?" I echoed, not having been paying attention. Papa blinked and repeated his request. Willie stepped back into the room at that moment, having helped Lily back to her room.

"Just some water," I croaked. "I'm really thirsty."

"We been gettin' you water every day," snorted Willie as he turned to run to the kitchen and fill a cup with clean water. I watched him go, smiling to myself. I had an incredible family, one that was willing to take care of me no matter what happened. Willie was part of that family now, whether he liked it or not! I shook my head quietly to myself, happily. I knew Willie liked it. He loved it.

Willie was more than happy to be part of our family. He loved our family – but I knew Lily was his favorite. I laughed aloud at the thought, just as Willie himself was jogging back in with the water.

He looked at me funny, but I ignored him and grabbed the cup.

"Water," I said lovingly, and poured almost all of it down my throat at once, spluttering. Willie and Papa watched, exchanging glances.

"Someone needed a drink," sang Willie.

Papa cackled and added, "of water, of course." They fell about croaking with laughter and I sat there, dumbfounded. Boys.

I felt so fond of my life, of my God. Despite the anger that sat malevolently in the back of my mind about Lily, I knew my God was for us. I pushed the resentment away. He'd literally pulled me through the storm, and I would be ever grateful for that. For all I knew, it had been God leading Willie to find me after the storm, God sending Willie to the barn to be safe in the first place. It made sense. The Lord I served took care of his children – we aren't slaves to him. We are royalty.

I made a face, thinking, 'Princess Alex,' and then Willie burst into laughter across from me.

"What on earth you doin'?" He said, guffawing. I pulled a wounded look.

"Nothing!" I said quickly. Then I muttered under my breath, "Laugh all you like, Willard. *I* am royalty, descended from the Most High."

Willie made a bemused face; apparently he'd heard me. Then he joined in. "Alex," he began, trying to speak proper, "I'm a prince too! We can rule the town! We can rule... the world!" He made a huge elaborate sweeping gesture at the word, 'world', and sat down, chuckling. I shook my head slowly, pretending to be hurt.

"How could you mock our lineage, Master Willard?" Said I, Princess Alex.

He sprung up from his seat instantly. "I wouldn't ever, dearest Princess, I were simply enjoyin' a sit-down." He tipped an imaginary hat and I giggled in a very lady-like manner.

Then I noticed Papa standing off to the side, watching us with an amused look on his face. I sighed huffily, "Master Willard, there is a peasant in our presence."

Willie turned with horror on his face and pointed. "Egads! Begone, ye of low birth!"

Papa put a hand to his chest and said, "Who, me? How dare ye! I am High Nobleman Jenkins!"

We all laughed and play-acted until I grew drowsy and fell asleep some time later, still with a smile on my face.

CHAPTER THIRTEEN

I had a lot of time to think and reflect while I was injured. I would lie on my couch and dream and consider, everything that had happened to me and my family flashing through my head. I had nothing much else to do when Papa and Willie were out working. I wasn't often still. This had been the first time I'd spent more than three days doing relatively nothing since I was really young. It felt bizarre.

I had been thinking about Mama a lot lately. I wasn't trying to be sad or anything, but sitting in the front room on the couch all day just brought back a lot of memories. I could envision her so easily sitting there next to me, braiding my hair or telling Lily and me a story. Mama loved to tell us stories. My favorite was about a beautiful girl who was very vain...

"Emeryl was always cruel and rude to anyone who was less beautiful than she, especially her younger sister Gwen, who had frizzy hair and a big nose and beady eyes," said Mama. She was sitting in between Lily and me, the firelight

dancing patterns over her face. Mama always made such dramatic expressions when she told stories. I loved her faces — they brought everything to life.

"To Emeryl, even Gwen's name was plain and unimpressive," Said Mama with sorrow in her voice, shaking her head slowly. "To Emeryl, beauty was everything. She based all of a person's worth on how they looked. But," Mama said slowly, looking at Lily and then looking at me, one eyebrow raised. "Do you know what happened?"

Lily giggled. "No, Mama!" I shook my head quickly, listening carefully and with an open mouth.

"Emeryl found out that she was the only one who saw herself as beautiful. Everyone else in the town had special eyes that saw someone's heart instead of their appearance, and they all knew how ugly she was inside." Mama said the word ugly with narrowed eyes and a clip in her voice, with suspense and drama portrayed in every movement she made, every hand gesture, with it written clearly over her face.

"When she found out, she wept and carried on and shouted at her father for lying to her for so long." Mama laced her fingers with Lily's and swept my hair out of my face.

"I know you two would never treat your father that way," She said, winking.

"No Mama, nooo," Said Lily, stuffing her pudgy little hands up against her face, gazing with serious eyes at Mama. Mama ruffled Lily's hair and continued.

"When Emeryl found out about the town and how they saw people, Gwen overheard her yelling at their father. Gwen took a look in the mirror and realized that she was truly beautiful – though on the outside, she was rough-looking, her heart was kind and good," said Mother with bright, sparkling eyes, "and the townsfolk knew her beauty. Gwen went to her sister and took her hand and cried, 'Emeryl! Come, sister. We can start anew. You can have beauty inside and out, if only you will treat others with less spite.'

But Emeryl would have none of it. 'Said the ugly duckling,' she sneered, yanking her arm away from Gwen's grip."

Mama's voice matched her dark hair as it fell over her face, and I thought about how beautiful my Mama was, even if it wasn't what mattered.

"And away Emeryl went – she was unhappy with her life in town, unhappy with these people who only saw inner beauty. Emeryl ran away, seeking vanity and shallowness – she went looking for others who valued outer appearances as highly as she did. And she was never heard from again." Mama said the last line, dropping her face and arms, closing her eyes with a dramatic coldness about her.

Lily squeaked and piped up, tugging at me, "Gawen," and I nodded.

"Mama, what happened to Gwen?"

Mama smiled at us each, then pointed at the fire. "As Gwen grew, she became more and more beautiful on the inside, and her wisdom was as sharp as the flames are hot. She became like a fire, giving warmth to all, offering beauty if one knew where to look." I tilted my head, trying to understand my mama's words. But even if I didn't understand the deeper meaning of the story, I loved it the most out of everything Mama told. It made me feel good, because I didn't base everything on my looks. I didn't even really know if I was beautiful on the outside, didn't quite care, but I knew I was on the inside, pretty at least, by the way Mama looked at me. And she'd taught me that inner beauty was all that mattered.

I was gazing off into the distance, transfixed by my memories of Mama. I realized that I was smiling stupidly at the wall and shook myself, lying down, yawning. Daydreaming could make you tired!

I lay there then, remembering something odd that had just popped into my head – It was right funny how the silliest little memories just stuck to you like glue sometimes. Mama had stayed with the Johanssons, our neighbors, for two weeks after their son died. When I was little, Papa told me it was 'cause they needed help getting over losing their only son. And I believed him. But now, I was thinking, how odd was it that Mama had stayed with them? For so long? After all, we were just neighbors. We weren't particularly close with them, never had been, they were an elderly couple and we were a young family. They mostly kept to themselves, though we exchanged dishes sometimes on holidays for the sake of being neighborly.

Right then Papa came in, clomping his feet at the door to get the dust off his boots. "Mornin', Alex," He said, rubbing his arm.

"It's not morning, Papa," I said absently.

He took off his hat and coat and hung them by the door. "You thinkin' bout somethin'? He asked as he walked through the kitchen.

"Yeah," I said. "Somethin'." Papa wandered away. Why would Mama stay with them? Why not somebody closer in relation to them? Then again, I reflected, there might not have been someone closer. The Johanssons didn't get out much, save to buy food and such. I shook my head, thinking how silly it was that I would read nonsense into such a situation. Mama was just being Mama when she helped those two elders out; she always did care more for others than for herself. I chided myself for ever even considering that something had been odd.

I was tired of lying around. I sighed and levered myself up off the couch. After days of healing, moving didn't hurt and I didn't get dizzy anymore when I stood slow enough. But I was stiff from lying still for so long, so I unbent myself and got up, stretching. I began to carefully make my way down the hallway. It felt good, stretching my muscles like this. It seemed as though I hadn't moved in absolute *ages*, compared to my usual non-stop hustle and bustle. I found myself wandering into my parents' room. I winced, mentally calling this place my parents' room when it was in fact singularly *Papa*'s room. Still, I eased in and sat on the side of the bed that used to be Mama's. I liked to believe that it still smelled like her in here.

THUMP!

Suddenly there was a huge sound from outside and behind me, and I jumped up to my feet in a flash. But outside was the least of my problems – my reflexes had launched me to my feet despite the fact that my brain couldn't move that fast. Shadows swept over me and moments later I found myself crumpled on the floor with a massive throb in my head. I groaned and pushed myself up slightly on my elbows. Suddenly a shimmer caught my attention. I was squarely in front of the old night stand Mama used to use, and underneath its carved bottom design piece was something gleaming in a shaft of sunlight.

I reached underneath it and my fingers brushed something solid and cold. I hesitated then moved my fingers around it, trying to pull it from the narrow space. The thing was stuck. Then I tugged sharply and the item grated out of its hiding spot, nicking the wood of the night stand on its way out. Then I was holding it – a beautiful silver frame with a faded picture inside.

I stared at it, confused. I was in the picture – with a boy I'd never seen before and a young man and woman who looked faintly familiar but did not spring any memories inside me. I was not very young in the photo; it looked to be only about three years ago.

You would remember this, I demanded to myself. *Who are those people?*

Suddenly footsteps sounded down the hall.

"Alex?" Called Papa. "You get anythin' to eat yet?" He was coming this way, calling for me. "Alex, where you got to?" For some irrational reason, I shoved the picture frame back where I'd found it and struggled to stand without falling again. Papa walked in just as I was settling myself back on the bed.

"Oh, there you are," he said with relief. "I was beginning to think you done gone crazy an' went outside, or somethin'," he said.

I just smiled and shook my head, saying, "You should have Willie make supper. I don't feel so well," I added.

Papa frowned. "Yeah, I weren't gonna make you do it." I just nodded faintly and slowly stood.

Papa looked at me narrowly. "You okay?"

I waved airily. "Fine, I just need some good food inside me, so Willie better prove to be a good enough cook tonight!" Papa chuckled and stepped aside to let me pass him as I made my very slow way back down the hall.

Willie called from the kitchen, "I can hear you all!"

I looked back at Papa quickly with mock terror on my face, gasping. Papa pretended to choke and I nodded, turning and making my way to the kitchen again.

"I understand, Papa," I said loudly. "You'd rather die than face a supper prepared by Willie!" I turned the corner and saw Willie boiling some water for stew. The broth was already smelling delicious from the onions and potatoes he'd tossed into it.

He had his nose in the air, refusing to make eye contact with me. "None for the likes o'you," He said, sniffing.

"Willie," I said with apologetic eyes, "your cooking is absolutely wonderful. Please don't cut me outta it!"

He turned, grinning, to me, and said, "I only wanted you t'say it out loud for me t'hear."

I snorted. "Yeah, well I only said it 'cause it's either eat horrid food or starve."

He lowered a brow over one eye at me, snorting. "Yer tellin' tales!" With that he turned and, without looking back, made a shooing motion with one hand. "Go on, git! I don't want no ingrates the likes o'you in here!"

"Ingrate?" I laughed. "Where'd you learn that word, Willie?"

He just shooed at me again. "Go on! Git! Outta here! G'bye!"

I limped back to my couch, laughing and coughing, my head aching. Boy, did supper smell good.

I had spent the past four days inside, goin' crazy. When I could, I got up and wandered around the house, bugging people. Whenever Willie was inside, I asked if I could help with the chores. When Papa came in, I asked if I could fix him any food. And either of them would always steer me back to the couch and make me sit down. I fumed at this – just because I was injured didn't mean I couldn't work! But Papa and Willie would have none of it. So the majority of those four days were spent on schooling. Whenever Lily was feeling up to it, I passed the time reading books to her in the melancholy atmosphere of her room. I had always been fantastic with words, but arithmetic was never my strong suit. Lily was better at working those problems.

Even with all that, though, I'd still spent some time alone, just sitting. The picture frame I'd found drifted into my mind. I didn't know what it was about it, but I couldn't stop wondering who the people were. I tried to convince myself that I was simply not recalling someone I'd been in a photo with –

but photos were rare enough, and it was unlikely that I'd taken a picture with someone I didn't know and then had forgotten all about it. I mused over the fact that the photograph had been faded. It must have been an old photo, much more so than three measly years! Nothing made sense right now.

Well, Papa and Willie still wouldn't let me go around doing any chores, so I decided I would go visit Lily. Maybe sing to her or something. I hadn't seen my Lil Flower yet today. Something in me ached for the old days, for the days when Lily and I had been care-free. I could barely remember them, those times when we'd gone out into the fields and played. I remembered coming in for supper to find Mama and Papa laughing like kids in the kitchen while Mama cooked and Papa tasted her food.

Those days were simpler – everything back then was better, it seemed. Lily hadn't been sick, I'd never been hurt, the dust storms didn't exist, Willie's Pa hadn't been dead, we were better off money-wise, and Papa smiled a lot more back then. But everything just got worse from there.

It started with the fire, and it started with the dust.

I shook the morbid thoughts from my head, going back to reminiscing. I remembered sitting down to eat as a family and always just inhaling the food like hungry dogs at the end of a long day. I remembered sitting with Mama for story time, Mama shooing Papa away and telling him she was telling stories to just the girls, Mama tracing the constellations with me, Mama showing me how to build a fire, Mama teaching me to braid hair, Mama taking care of me when I was sick, Mama kissing Lily's cuts to make them better, Mama and Papa dancing together at a Festival long ago.

I remembered Mama, and the days when she was with us. I missed those days.

I hefted myself up and began the seemingly endless trek down the hallway to Lily's room. When Papa went into town last, he had gone to speak to the town doctor. Papa had gone asking about Lily, wondering when she would get better and if there was anything we could do to speed up her healing.

But the doctor had shaken his head at the word, *"healing"*. He'd stopped Papa, saying, "Healing? I don't think you understand, sir." Then he'd hesitated.

Papa had looked at him closely, asking, "What do you mean?"

The Doctor had pushed his glasses up onto his nose with a regretful finger and then turned to face Papa. "Do you forget? Your daughter had Polio."

Papa'd sighed. "How could I forget? Ain't a day goes by I don't a'member."

The doctor had shrugged at Papa's annoyance and delivered the rest of the news in one fell swoop. "Most people *don't* recover from Polio."

CHAPTER FOURTEEN

I was yanked back to the present in a painful and abrupt manner as I stumbled and fell in the hallway. I had tripped and then lay sprawled on the floor, head wound aching, lungs itching. I tried to roll over and groaned, my body hurting. Why, why did I allow myself to get lost in daydreams? Nothing good ever came of it.

I didn't want Willie or Papa to rescue me again, or find me lying on the floor, so I rose from the ground as quickly as I found possible. I pulled on the walls as I stood. Hardly any darkness flashed before me, so I couldn't have damaged myself much more than I already was. I almost laughed at that – damaged goods! That was what I was now.

But then Lily flashed into my mind and all merriment vanished from inside me. I suddenly felt very, very depressed and sad, completely fed up with Lily being crippled. It was unfair and cruel. I had to wonder why God had allowed it to happen – surely there was no purpose for this.

Just then a memory of Mama flashed into my mind.

"People say that God has a purpose for making everything happen," Said Mama. "They say that we just don't understand it always."

I was sitting next to her, sewing pockets on an old dress of mine. Her voice was soft and thoughtful.

"I don't agree with them, though, Alexandria," She said, shaking her head. Long waves of silk tumbled from her scalp and floated with her movement. I wanted my Mama's hair – I have always wanted my Mama's hair. Instead I have been stuck with the dusty mop I have.

"Why, Mama? Why don't you agree?" My voice was high and sharp, youthful and almost annoying in its tones.

Mama reached over to take my hand and clasped it between both of hers. "Think about it, dear one," She said, giving my hand a light squeeze.

"Is our Father powerful enough to do as He pleases?" She asked me, awaiting my answer carefully.

"Yes, Mama, God can do what He likes."

"And does He like to hurt people and take their lives away?"

I thought of the times He had helped me and my friends, and shook my head firmly.

"So if God doesn't like hurting people, and He can do what he likes, why would He ever hurt someone?" I didn't quite understand, but I loved hearing my Mama talk and pretending I was smart and old enough to have a conversation with her.

"He wouldn't?" I ventured.

Mama smiled and tapped me on the nose. "Exactly, my little dear one. God doesn't cause bad things to happen – sin and broken people and life in general in this fallen world do that. Therefore all things have a reason for happening, but all things do NOT have a purpose. Not at the beginning, anyhow. But God does take bad events and things and make good out of the ashes, so that they are not in vain. He gives them a purpose." She said.

Now I thought I understood. God didn't make bad things happen because He had a purpose for them to occur – but He turned bad things around after sin, darkness, free will, and a fallen world had been the reason they happened. I knew He protected us from lots of bad things that we never even knew about.

By now, I had been standing in the door of Lily's room for quite some time. I heard coughing inside and ventured through the dark doorway. Suddenly I heard Lily cry out, half coughing, half hoarse yelling.

"Mama!" She called, crying in relief. "Mama!" I choked on the air and spun around, wanting to leave. This hadn't happened in quite some time. I hadn't been prepared.

I'd forgotten that Lily often confused me for Mama. I didn't quite understand it, really. I supposed that in the darkness, Lily saw only my face structure and that I incredibly resembled Mama at moments like that. Mama used to be tall and fair-skinned, and I was shorter and very tan. Mama'd had long, beautiful dark hair, and I had a curly mat of dusty blond.

But in the shadows, to confused eyes... I could understand the resemblance between my Mama and me. I rushed to Lily's side.

"No, Lil. I'm so sorry. It's me, Alex, it's me." I said, sorrow cracking my voice every few words. Lily stopped wailing out and stared at me in confusion.

"Alex?" Lily said my name. Not Oxie. Alex. So much disappointment in that one word.

She squinted and crossed her eyes and tried to see Mama where I now stood, but she couldn't, and she gave up trying.

That was when the crying began. Oh, did it claw darkness into my soul.

Every sob, every heart-wrenching gasp for air, left *me* aching inside and wishing that it had been Mama come to see Lily instead of me. Lily turned and buried her face in the bed, trying to stop the tears. And the worst kind they were – that of an innocent, disappointed girl. A child's tears were bad enough, they could make anyone feel terrible, but a broken child whose Mama had gone long ago, without ever saying goodbye?

Every part of me felt sick with sadness. Here was my sister, weeping in the darkness of a dusty room, because I looked like my mother. I cursed myself for bringing these tears on her. I stroked her hair and began to sing.

"Hush little baby, don't you cry,
You've gotta be brave for another night.
Hush little darling, don't be so sad,
Mama loves you so and she misses you bad."

Lily finally calmed down, and I felt weak with relief. Her crying literally sapped my strength – I felt more drained now than ever before. More sick, more tired, more lifeless. I had lost hope here and now, in this moment. But I wasn't going to stop moving, wasn't going to stop believing, even if I'd stopped hoping.

Hope and faith are two very different things, you see. Hope is trying to make yourself happy when things are terrible; hope is wishing for something to smile about when you have nothing. Hope is wanting something to look forward to through the darkness. But faith, faith is completely different. Asking someone to hope and asking someone to have faith require different things of a person. To have faith is much harder than simply hoping – even though sometimes, when one has nothing left, sometimes faith is all there is. I felt like that about then.

I didn't have any hope left – no rational belief said that anything would ever be okay again. Rationality said that hope was dead.

I was sad, and tired, and sick of hoping. Yet I still had faith. Faith gives one more than hope, I like to believe. Because to have faith, you must believe that the Lord will help you persevere. Hope is just a notion – just a thought to keep from despair, albeit a good and decent thing – while faith is believing beyond the rational. Hope is a thought, an idea, a fragile desire. Faith is solid trust, belief, knowledge. Beyond logic and rationality stands faith. And once you do believe that the Lord will sustain you, once you believe in God's master plan, once you have faith in His hand over everything, well, you can rest assured that the world won't consume you.

CHAPTER FIFTEEN

It had been a full five days after my accident when I decided that I was done lying around. I wanted to go back to the fields.

I wanted to go back to the fields. I never thought I would want such a thing. But after almost a week of being helpless, useless, and a burden on my family, I was fed up with doing nothing. It was time I earned my keep again, and that did not include lying on the couch counting the days as they passed.

The dizziness and nausea had almost completely left me now; I could get up and move around without danger of passing out. Well, for the most part, anyway. I could walk and move carefully enough just fine. I was determined to get up and do something productive, like supper, dishes or sweeping. Come to think of it, I wanted to do everything.

It was a Monday morning, after all. Willie and Papa were in town, and I was alone in the house with Lily. She wasn't gonna tell me not do some chores! Actually, Lily was still sleeping, and would probably doze til late morning. When she did get up, she could help me fold clothes or do the dishes.

I paused for a moment to think about how Lily was doing. She could be convinced to get up and sit in the living room to do simple tasks with a little prodding. Some days were worse than others. The pain in her leg would dictate whether she'd get up or not. I could usually tell the night before if she'd be able to do chores the next day – she'd cry out in the night, through dark terrors that searched for her. I feared that the ghosts of her once-healthy body would never stop haunting her.

Lily's nightmares weren't like mine; they didn't revolve around death and heartache and dust. Her darkest dreams were the embodiment of her fear, that she'd never again live a normal life. I had heard and seen the effects of these dreams. I believed that her thrashing in the night was due to the ever-present ache in her broken body, due to this lingering darkness that thrived in her bones.

I snapped myself out of the gloomy shadows of my mind and looked around. I was standing in the kitchen, feeling confused. It was just beginning to grow light out, the sun creeping slowly over the horizon. Listening, I heard soft breathing from Lily's room. Reassurance flooded like a gentle wave through my veins, and my shoulders dropped. The anxious pumping of my heart relaxed. There was no use dwelling on things that I couldn't help. I would continue to pray for my family and for Lily – and today I'd let her sleep. Aside from that, there wasn't much I could do for her.

Now there was work to be done. I headed for the back porch and the electric washtub. First I dumped a pile of dirty clothes into the tub and filled it with buckets of water from the well. Thankfully, our farm was equipped with a deep, clean well where we got all our water. Papa had built a windmill years ago with the help of some men from town. It pumped water up with the breeze, which was strong here on the plains. Although there was no rain and the drought had been going on for some time, we had drinking water in plenty for our family. We did try to use it sparingly where other needs were concerned.

The tub groaned and shook as it cleaned our clothing, and then I cranked each piece through the rods. After I'd wrung most of the water out, I clipped the laundry up on the clothesline. Once I was done with the work, I left the water in the washtub. We'd use it again later. The sun moved a bit farther up the sky. Next was the sweeping of the house.

I went inside, my back aching from bending. I felt sort of weak and shaky and realized that I'd forgotten to eat yet that morning. I headed straight for the kitchen and ate what leftovers we had from the night before. Stew was pretty delicious like this, cold and thick.

I sighed as I took a last spoonful of potatoes and carrots, and then I put my dishes away. I still had a lot to do before

Willie and Papa got home, and it was almost noon. I had overestimated my ability to work quickly in this state, when every move carried a trace of pain, or a stiff ache that lingered to make me more aware of the work I was doing. It was hard to get into the rhythm of work and let the hours slip by when I was brought back to reality every moment by annoying twinges of soreness. The laundry had already taken me quite a bit of time and effort, and I was tired. But I was determined to finish these few chores, at least. I went to get the broom from the porch and then headed for the back rooms to sweep.

As I walked, my mind crafted images of possibilities that I craved. I imagined all of our lives becoming easier. Money being less tight, the dust storms ceasing, us picking up and moving to the city, and Willie going with us...

I stopped dead in shock. The thoughts had just been flowing through my brain without me thinking much about them, but... had I really just imagined moving to the city? Surely I didn't *want* to go there, did I? Not deep inside myself, or anything? I frowned, very disturbed. I loved my home here, my life here. Wasn't it good enough for me anymore?

A tiny voice inside me whispered, *Maybe you could go to school in the city.*

I swallowed a lump in my throat. I had dropped out of school long ago because Papa needed help around here. Lily had never gone much, only for a few months, really. She had just begun going when Mama went away, and then she wouldn't go anymore. I didn't blame her. Most of the children there *had* mothers... and for weeks after the accident, people had looked at us with... with pity in their eyes, but mostly with relief. *Relief.* As if our pain was a reminder to them that *hey,* at least they still had a mama! I swallowed. I didn't want to think about this now. Not school, not Mama. Not the fact that I was so, so terrified of losing Papa, of becoming an orphan like Willie...

I bit my lip and looked down, forcing myself to stop thinking about it. I stepped inside Mama and Papa's room stiffly, feeling bitter with pain and sorrow, my motivation to clean vanishing like dew in the morning sun.

I walked around to the side of the bed and sat down dismally, leaning the broom against the wall. My eyes drifted slowly to the nightstand, and my blood stirred as I thought of what was hiding underneath. Standing slowly, I turned toward the nightstand. With measured movements, as if I were afraid that anything too fast might startle my goal away, I lowered myself to my hands and knees and reached under the nightstand. I suddenly felt an intense, eager longing for the frame, for the mystery of the faded photograph.

My fingers touched cold darkness, nothing more.

Completely and utterly confused, I sat back on my heels, staring at the space between the nightstand and the floor. It wasn't very big – there was nowhere the frame could have gone. Slowly a truth trickled into my mind; that someone must have moved the frame. Regret began to seep sluggishly through my veins, with all the sureness of a stalking predator. I was aware only of the fact that I felt an odd and fierce protective nature over the lost object, and that I felt it unfair to have something of such great value simply snatched away from me.

I paused and pondered this a moment. I considered the frame to be worth much, yet it was just an old piece of metal, nothing actually of value. My mind must have made some sort of connection to the frame and the photo; something was there, something that meant a whole awful lot, but I just couldn't quite grasp what the entire thing meant. Thinking about the photo made my mind hurt. For some reason, our neighbors' faces popped into my mind. They'd been around a long while. Maybe they knew something of the picture? But that was silly, I reflected. I could just ask Papa.

Some dark hesitation coiled around me as I considered talking to Papa about the frame. It felt... wrong. Like this was none of my business, even though it was. I just shook my head and stood up, lifting the broom once again. My mind was twitching and misfiring, trying to remember something, trying to put together a puzzle of which I didn't quite have all the pieces.

Finally I gave up and found myself making my way down the hall, sweeping. This photograph business didn't make any sense, and dwelling on it, without having it to actually examine, would just drive me straight to frustration. I put all my annoyance into my work, finishing the sweeping a lot earlier than I'd have thought. I decided the floors were plenty clean and put off mopping. I leaned against the kitchen counter, wondering. What else had I to do? I was pretty sure that the midday meal and dishes were all that was left. If I tried to do anything else that had to do with the animals or the crops, I'd get a right proper lashing of the tongue when Papa got home. So I focused on making a good meal.

Lily ate whatever I made for her. Sometimes her throat was raw from coughing and she didn't want food, but I didn't like how thin she was, so those days I'd get her to manage some cornbread soaked in milk. I was pretty sure she ate it just to get me to stop nagging. I was just glad that she was eating, because honestly, she didn't have anywhere else to get nutrients. Lily didn't have any fat for her body to chew. Just lil old Lily, withering away, with her twisted limbs and tired soul. I tried not to think about it as I prepared, yet again, stew.

It was a good supper, and nobody ever complained, though Willie oft made faces as he faced our repetitive meal. "Stew again!" he'd say. I usually just ignored him and rolled my eyes. Papa was always careful to casually compliment the cook, so as to ensure that somebody always wanted to make supper. It was like he was tryin' to train us. He'd been doing that for a long time, though back when Mama was around, he complimented her just 'cause he loved her, and he loved her cooking.

I sighed absently and kept stirring my project. The days were beginning to blur together, and the frame I'd found had offered a brief respite to the monotony. Had I just imagined what I'd seen? After all, I'd only gotten a quick look at it in a darkened room, and I'd put it back quickly enough when I heard Papa coming. Then it had vanished completely! Perhaps I was just hallucinating from being ill in the head for so long.

Beginning to hum some mostly forgotten tune, I chopped some chives up and dropped them into the stew pot. I sniffed appreciatively as the lovely aromas of melding ingredients wafted toward me in a thick white sheet of vapor. The steam rising from the stew drifted with a breeze cutting through my house and assaulted my face, filling my lungs with moisture. I breathed it appreciatively.

"Do I smell food cookin'?" called someone from the other room. The front door slammed. It sounded like Papa.

"Only enough for me," I yelled back. Papa came clunking into the kitchen.

"You've got the grace of an elephant, d'you know that?" I informed him insolently. Papa just snorted and ruffled my hair with a dusty hand. I clucked unappreciatively and moved away, not wanting dust in my hair, even though my tangled curls were the *color* of dust. I chuckled at myself, grinning.

Papa looked up at me from where he'd been gazing longingly into the pot. "Whatcha snortin' at, Alex?" He wondered at my smile. I sniffed at him.

"Better check your nose," I said slowly. "I just found it in my business!" I fell about cackling at his did-you-really-just-say-that expression. Willie strolled into the kitchen nice and slow then, lookin' tired and actually quite a bit tanner.

"Willie!" I yelped. "You're not pasty anymore!"

Willie looked mournfully at the back of his arm. "I know, ain't it awful," he said. I made a face at him and he cracked a smile.

"A'ight," Said Papa, no longer able to wait, "Let's git to eatin'." With that, he swooped in with a bowl and scooped some stew up before moving toward our small kitchen table. Willie whooped and grabbed a dish, but I smacked him on the hand with my ladle before he got very far.

"Yowch," he said, putting the bowl down to rub his hand. "What was that fer?"

"Nothing at all," I said, matching his nasally tone perfectly. He narrowed his eyes and raised one brow.

"Alright, alright, keep your clogs on," I muttered, turning to lift Lily's bowl carefully from the counter next to me.

"This is a powerful antidote that will cure Lily's hunger instantly. Bear it to her with goodwill and care, for it is the last of its kind." Willie nodded his head stoically and saluted before beginning his long march into infected territory. I could only hope that he should ever return.

While Willie was gone, I quickly filled a bowl for myself and sat down across from my Papa, trying to find words for what I wanted to say. He kept looking up at me with a weird expression on his face. Finally he sat up straight, dropping the spoon into his bowl with a *klunk*.

"Whatcha got on your mind, Alex? You ain't taken a bite o' that, and y'keep starin' at me." I started nervously; I still hadn't decided what to say. "Um..."

Papa rubbed his eyes and looked at me dramatically. "Really? That's right intrestin'."

I felt instantly annoyed. "I found a silver frame with an old faded photo inside and I think the picture is Mama when she was little, with her parents."

The revelation was odd, seeing as it had tumbled from my mouth without any prior conscious thought, but I realized it made sense. That would explain everything! The mystery of the photo frame, solved. But Papa just looked at me with wide eyes and open mouth until Willie returned, then Papa began to eat again. Without ever answering my question.

CHAPTER SIXTEEN

Finally, it was time to return to work on the farm.

I could work again. I was healed enough to do some weeding. No plowing or heavy work to do right now – just weeding. I could kneel in the dirt and use my hands for a few hours, no problem.

I was so incredibly relieved to be of use again, I almost completely forgot about the fact that Papa had brushed me off completely a couple days before while we were eating. As I headed outside, dressed for my work, I resolved that I would corner Papa and make him tell me what the old photo of Mama and her parents was hiding. There was something odd about the whole thing. Now that I'd figured out that it wasn't me in the photo, it should be perfectly ordinary. Just a picture. But the fact that Papa moved it from its place under the nightstand, combined with his shocked silence at lunchtime, convinced me that there was something more here. So what was the photo hiding?

Mama and Papa had never lied to us. If it wasn't a lie, then what *was* all this business with the photo? I had never been directly lied to about it, because Papa had never spoken of it. So did that make it more of a hidden truth than a lie? I hadn't known of its existence until just days before. Yet there was some sort of secret hanging over the photo like a storm cloud. I hadn't imagined the pale fear in my papa's face. Was my family hiding something significant?

I shook myself. What on earth was I doing? This was all just me over-thinking a simple situation again. Papa probably just hadn't heard me, that was all. And he moved the frame cause he'd found it right after me, and it didn't belong where it was. I rationalized every speculation that I'd come up with, and soon enough I was pulling weeds in the hot sun, with my mind completely on my work. All I was thinking about was how wilted the crops looked... The corn stalks were coming up much slower than usual, and who knew how the potatoes were doing. Last we'd checked, they were small and unimpressive. I sighed and kept pulling unwanted weeds from our fields.

Without thinking of anything but the dirt before me and the plants I was caring for, I spent two hours yanking tough stems from the land. I had just finished the biggest plot of ground and as I got up and dusted myself off, the hair on the back of my neck stood up. I stiffened and slowly turned around.

On the horizon behind me was a giant mass of roiling darkness that was sweeping toward our farm. Fast.

At the sight of what had nearly cost me my life barely two weeks before, everything inside me shut down. I dropped to the ground and my blood turned to ice. I was shivering. There was a heaviness in my gut, a despair that dragged me down. It anchored my flesh to this oncoming doom.

The darkness came closer.

My teeth chattered violently. I needed to get up! To move! To run to the house! I tried, I really did. I pushed my shaking hands into the ground and tried to lever myself up on them, but my arms were like noodles. I just collapsed on my face, trembling.

Mere miles stood between me and the dust. Panic rushed through my veins – I couldn't be out in this again! This wasn't fair! I wouldn't last through something so terrible again! No one would come for hours... Willie and Papa had left for the market early that morning, and they'd told me that it may be long past midday before they made it home.

I felt so afraid – so full of terror. I was petrified. *You won't make it through this,* I thought to myself. I just knew. *This is it.*

The fear melted into my soul and formed an icy calm. What if I died here? So what? I could be with Mama again...

The calm pounded in my bones. *Give in,* it whispered. *It's over.* I felt the temptation to let go wavering in my chest like an emotion that wasn't sure of its own identity. *Am I calm in this moment?* I thought. *Am I letting go? Time to sleep,* I thought tiredly. The wave rolled closer, and its hissing embrace called softly to relinquish the fight...

Agony wormed inside me like a sudden burst of flame as I realized what was happening. I was listening to the darkness. Now was not the time to die. Not for me. Not like this. My life wasn't over simply because I couldn't *get up and move!* I looked behind me. The storm looked to be less than a mile away now, shooting through the land with deadly chaos.

I stood.

I ran.

Adrenaline pumped through my blood, I felt it shake my ribs, and I ran. I ran as I had never run before, my soul crying out to live, to survive. There was nothing like death to remind you how much you wanted to live.

I kicked up enough dust to start a storm myself as I bolted for home. I was yards away from the front door, feet, minutes, seconds, and moments. I looked behind me and tasted the dust, felt it as it reached out for me; then I was through, into the house. I slammed the front door shut and latched it, and then I slumped against it, fighting for breath. I was choking on air; there wasn't enough oxygen to pull into my lungs. I rasped and wheezed and felt my chest ache with terrible emptiness.

Slowly my breath returned, but the dust came with it. I felt like an ant beside the enormity of the storm. Giant, vengeful hands grabbed our house in their swirling embrace, and I felt the impact through the shuddering wood. Suddenly dust was shooting through the cracks and fissures of the house, whisking into our home and tainting our air with poison.

I coughed and crawled away from the entrance, hacking. All I felt in those moments was an intense longing for clean air. No worry for my family, for the crops, for the animals. Just selfish want for air.

My eyes were watering buckets. I breathed through my shirt and looked around in near-panic. I couldn't see anything, couldn't hear a sound but the rushing of the dust. I could no longer feel it coming under the door. That was odd. The dust had never piled up on the door before. I wondered if it was blowing in a different direction. So thick was the darkness that I was almost sure my eyes had ceased to function; how could anything hide the sun as this storm had? The shadows were thick, terrible, and absolute.

I lifted my head, eyes straining, and stood up shakily...Lily! I had to see that Lily was alright. Coughing and choking, I stumbled through the black, eyes shut against the dust.

Somehow, I made it to Lily's room. Staggering in, I called out to her. I thought I heard her answer me, but it was hard to tell. I stuck my hands in front of me, trying to find the bed. Almost there...

My hands hit the wall, and I jerked my eyes open in confusion, trying to see. Still nothing. Turning in toward the room again, I tried to reach her bed. My hands gripped blankets and my shins banged against a wooden frame.

"Lily!" I called out, but it felt like my mouth was stuffed with cotton. I could barely hear my own voice.

A muffled response drifted tantalizingly through my mind. Had I actually heard anything, or was I inventing what I wanted to hear? It was hard to tell with the hissing storm around me. I lifted myself up onto the bed, crawling forward, seeking. Then I found a small bundle curled tightly under what felt like heaps of blankets. *Lily.*

I put my face close to her and tried to make my voice heard, "I'm here!"

Suddenly I felt a hand grab my arm. I held on to it tightly.

And there we sat, for the longest time, through the dust and darkness. Then silence. An echoing, static-filled quiet that smelled like sunlight and dirt.

Had the storm gone? Everywhere, darkness still reigned. I held Lily's hand tightly, trying not to be afraid. We were bathed in an absolute void of light. I didn't know how long the shadows would last. At some point, I began to doubt that the light would ever return – the darkness was so absolute, and so dirty. The taste and smell of soil assaulted me with every breath. We weren't even safe here, in our home. We wouldn't ever be safe from the dust.

I must have dozed off, because next thing I knew, there was banging and yelling.

"Alex! Lily, are you in there!"

I started and opened my eyes. Weak, hazy sunlight was filtering in all around us, and the sound of shuddering blows came from the front room. Someone was pounding on the door. It took a moment for me to register that my name was being called, and that I needed to get up. I struggled up, releasing Lily's hand. She seemed to be awake.

"Are you alright?" I asked her. I could see her through the dirty air, and she nodded, rubbing her eyes. So I turned and stumbled through the hall, reaching the door, which was latched. As I reached to unhook the door, I shook my head, oddly amused at my own proclivity to lock out the storm. I pushed against the solid timber, but it wouldn't move.

"I'm here!" I yelled. "But I can't open the door!"

I heard a muffled exhalation from the other side, followed by words that I couldn't make out.

Then Papa's voice was back. "Alex, it's me 'n Willie," yelled Papa. "We gotta git this dust away from th' door. You sit tight an' we'll get to clearin' it." I barely had time to shout, "Okay!" before the voices faded.

I waited in silence for their return, and jumped when loud thumps suddenly sounded from outside.

Scccrrrraaaape.. clunk! Scccrrrraaaaape.. The shovels made hollow sounds, hitting the door and scooping up the grit. I relaxed and waited. After a few minutes, the sounds stopped, and the door swung open.

"Alex!" yelled Willie as he ran in to hug me. Papa looked over me quickly and then ran back toward Lily's room.

"We was pretty scared for you," Willie admitted. "When th' storm hit, all's I could think was, 'Is Alex inside, or will I have t' drag her home on a sack again?'" He was half-joking, but I heard the fear in his voice. He really had been afraid for me.

A sudden wave of affection swept over me, and I punched Willie in the arm.

"I *was* outside when it came, Willie, but I ran like you on Festival Day goin' after free sweets," I said. He rubbed his arm and shook his head, walking past me toward the hall.

"How's the Lil Monster?" He asked, as Papa rushed by us again and out the door.

"She's okay. I was with her through most o' the storm." I looked at Willie and saw the worry still in his eyes. We turned as one and walked down the hall to Lily's room. She was sleeping peacefully, so we didn't wake her, returning instead to the kitchen. Willie looked relieved.

"We gotta clean out all this... this," he said, gesturing at the dust blanket that covered everything. I nodded absently as I stared out the open front door. *Was it worse than last time?*

Willie and I looked at each other then, as the dust drifted down in a golden haze through the air. His expression reflected my own dread. Swallowing hard, I led the way out the door, and then we were running. We coughed as we stomped through the tinted air. After the last storm, quite a percentage of the crops had been damaged, but we still had just about enough to make it through the year. Had this storm been any longer or more vicious than the last?

It felt as though I was always running. Earlier I'd run away from the fields – to the safety of home – now I was running back, scared for our crops, for my family. I reached the devastation in minutes, with Willie not too far behind. Papa was standing on the edge of the fields, with his hands on his knees and his head hanging low. Willie caught up to me, panting. Then he slowed down, taking in the masses of shored-up dirt before us.

I turned away from the scene, turned to Willie. "The crops are dead."

CHAPTER SEVENTEEN

We spent the next four hours clearing excess soil away from our lands. The crops were gone, choked and buried under soil. It seemed so unreal. This was our livelihood, our only source of food and security and money.

Gone.

Like anything good in my life, I thought bitterly. Nothing pure lasted here. Nothing less than evil thrived. I pushed away the enraged tears that rose behind my eyes and kept shoveling death away from the ground before me, kept clearing the soil away from the few living plants left. Our corn stalks, with most of the plant being exposed, had never stood a chance. Nearly all of them were shredded and dead or dying. Most of our crops had been corn – the seeds are cheaper to buy – and now only the potatoes had survived. Our hopes for the potatoes were already wilting, and things would surely only get worse from here. I passed a rotting, shredded cornstalk and glared at it with frustration. It seemed like one storm was coming after another. Just when my family had come up for air, something shoved us under the water again.

How could we possibly survive?

This was all that we had. Dark talk had been circulating around town, spinning predictions of further bad fortune to come. Papa had been bringing news of awful things occurring further east that seemed like nightmares. He talked of lands succumbing to huge and distorted numbers of rabbits, insects that swarmed in devastating mobs, and raging disease caused and spread by the dust. Fear trickled through my chest. Lily was getting sicker, most of our crops were gone, I had just recovered from a severe head injury, and now things were going to worsen? How could there possibly be more?

The panic grew in my head until I closed my eyes and pressed my hands against my ears. I couldn't do this. Not now, not here. Bending down to clear off some stalks that had a shred of life in them still, I took a deep breath and focused everything on the task at hand. I was good at that, forgetting the world and pretending the only thing that mattered was whatever I was doing at the moment.

Forgetting the world. My other responsibilities, my worries, my anxieties. Forgetting them. It felt pretty good. But it was oh, so selfish.

I bit the inside of my cheek and continued my work. *Stop thinking, Alex,* I commanded myself. *Breathe in, breathe out. Work. Breathe, work. Breathe, work.* After a few moments of mental command, I was a machine. I could do this. Breathe, work.

Nothing could be easier.

I followed my mantra for hours. We were focusing on a section of our land that was less covered, shoveling away the soil. Time blended and flew by, only marked by my progressively worse back pain and how my hands began to bleed. I bent to clear more dirt away, reaching...

"Alex, ain't nothin' more t'do today." A strong hand clamped down on my shoulder. I stood, a dazed light in my eyes. Papa was looking at me with narrowed eyes and an odd expression. Then he stepped back and lifted his head.

"Go on in and get cleaned up now, y'hear," He said slowly, his accented twang sounding odd with such a serious tone.

"We two's gonna go on an' finish the chores for today." He hooked a thumb at Willie and they turned to the barn and the pens. I turned, slumped, and made my way to the house. I barely even remembered it when I wiped the dirt off my hands and arms with a washcloth, too tired to fill the bath.

The next thing I knew, I was sitting at the kitchen table. My thoughts weren't conscious. I was hardly aware of anything but a buzzing in my ears. Suddenly Papa and Willie were sitting next to me, mouths forming words. I just looked at them blankly. I narrowed my eyes in focus and suddenly I heard Papa speaking.

"Times are gettin' tougher, sure 'nough," he said, swallowing. "We all gotta belt up n' do our best with what we got."

I listened with half-lidded eyes. Papa took a deep breath. "A'fore we lose all hope completely," he put his hands up on the table, outstretched, reaching, "let's git to prayin'. Ain't nothin' else to do t'day. Best way to stop feelin' sorry for y'self is to pray."

He nodded at Willie, and Willie slipped his hands into mine and Papa's. Then Papa grabbed my other hand, and we all closed our eyes. I heard my heart thumping hard in my ears. I felt awake again.

"Lord, we don't know what t'do," said Papa, an audible tremor in his voice. "We're afraid, and we're hurtin', 'n we're pretty darn mad at ya, too." He swallowed thickly. "Now, I don't 'spose none of us will ever unnerstand exactly what's goin' on here, or why all this is happenin' to us. We don't now 'n prob'ly never will." Papa was speaking with his words slippin' together.

He slid into his accent more when he was really upset. "But right now," Papa said slowly, squeezing my hand, "we're choosin' t' have faith. We wanna come out o' this situation in whatever way you want us to, even if it don't make sense to us.

S'long as we're listenin', Father, we know you'll show us the way to go. So please. We're listenin' – don't leave us. We got a lotta questions and a lotta prayers. Please start answerin' them."

He broke off, voice shaking and head down. I felt huge sympathy swelling up inside me. My Papa was trying to provide for his broken family, and he was havin' the toughest time just getting food on the table. Not to mention he'd welcomed a lost orphan boy into his already struggling family with open arms.

"Well," said Papa hastily, rising from the table and scrubbing at his eyes, "that's done with, then. Ya'll know He heard us," He added convincingly. "He's got some kind o' plan in place. Just gotta have faith," He echoed Mama's favorite saying in a half-hearted way.

She'd always said that when something didn't quite go how we wanted it to. *"He's got a plan in place, we just gotta have faith."* And she'd always smile reassuringly and wipe away our tears...

I sniffled, missing Mama now more than ever. I looked up quickly at Willie. He was staring at the table with his hands hanging by his sides. I tilted my head. Something was off with him. I didn't quite know what, but honestly, it wasn't my business just now. If Willie wanted to talk, he'd talk. Besides, I had plenty of my own secrets to unravel. I left him staring forlornly at the wooden table and slipped quietly down the hall after Papa.

His door was shut. I went to knock on it – "Papa?" – but it just swung wide open. And there was Papa, sitting on Mama's side of the bed with the silver frame in hand. Gazing at it. And there were tears in his eyes.

He didn't look up as I entered the room and stood before him. "Papa?" I said quietly, hardly wanting to disturb him, but struggling with curiosity that was spiraling out of control.

He kept right on starin' at that photo, sighing. "She were so selfless," Papa said softly. "Always wantin' life t'be fair, always wantin' everybody t'get a second chance." He smiled sadly with his eyes, shaking his head ever so slightly. I stood rooted to the spot.

Papa looked up at me, waving the photograph. "When you was a little'un, you took one o' Lily's favoritest dolls right from under her nose, and you jus' wasn't gonna give it back." Then he laughed, and for some reason I felt a bittersweet sorrow turning sharply inside me like a knife. "So yore mama goes an' tells you a story 'bout when she were growin' up, and how her brother set flame t'her best dress. 'Bout how sad she were, how she wished she were able t'wear it again, but it were gone. How long she cried 'bout losin' it." I just listened, not remembering any of this. Mama had never talked about her brother when I was older. I had always assumed she'd left him behind when she moved here.

Papa smiled a real smile now. "Youse gave 'er that doll right quick, mutterin', 'Sissie, I's sorry, don't cry,'" over and over again until Lily quit sniffling." I frowned, feeling sicker by the moment. Papa was like a lost man without Mama. He missed their life together so much. It was the worst thing I'd ever seen, ever been through. Two people who loved each other that much – one of them forced to keep on livin' while the other went away forever.

Well, not forever, I thought, blinking slowly. Papa was staring into his photograph again.

I began to speak before I realized what I was doing. "Papa, what's the great big secret about that photo? Why'd you act like I'd poured oil on your head when I asked about it?"

He looked at me, and something flickered in his eyes. "I don't right know what youse talkin' 'bout," he said coldly. Suddenly Papa's eyes were harsh and unforgiving. I shrank away, frightened.

"But Papa–"

He broke through my sentence, waving a hand. "You git now."

I stared at him, openmouthed. "But..."

He was already gazing off into his photograph again. I didn't even exist in that moment. Angry, I stormed away, slamming his door shut behind me. As I stomped down the hall and slumped dejectedly onto the couch, I thought sorely of my failure. I felt so close, so close to finding out the secret that I knew existed. I didn't doubt it anymore. There was something here, something solid and real, something Papa was hiding, but for what reason, I didn't know.

I thought about how I could find any further information. Obviously Papa wasn't going to tell me anything. He was protective of something and I wanted to know what it was. Everything inside me yearned to understand just what was so secret about my Mama's past and her parents. I thought about the photo. There had been a little boy in the picture – had that been Mama's brother?

I shook my head, confusing myself. I was just going in circles here. I couldn't be sure of anything without the photo and someone to explain it to me. Stumped, I stared at the empty fireplace, willing answers to jump into my frenzied mind. All my thoughts were swirling around like a tempest, tangling up and tearing and making no sense at all!

Frustrated all over again, I took a deep breath and thought about it. Mama had moved here with her family, I assumed, so people somewhere should have known her parents and her siblings, if she had any. There had to be *someone* in this town willing to tell me about Mama's family.

I thought hard. Who did I know that was old enough to have known Mama when she was younger? I thought of the townsfolk... all of my teachers from my schooling days were too young, not many years removed from how old Mama would be right now. I would need someone who'd been around here awhile, like an older couple.

Of course, I thought, relieved. *I'll go visit the Johanssons.*

CHAPTER EIGHTEEN

As I pulled the pie from the oven, I breathed in the heavy scent of buttered crust and sugared apples. It looked delicious, baked with the last of the green apples off the tree that grew behind our home. It was small, though. We didn't quite have the reserves to go baking big pies willy-nilly. I'd preserved these apples for an occasion. Some time when we'd use them, for a celebration, maybe a birthday.

I paused. When was my birthday again? A few months? I felt numb. I would be fourteen in a few months. Had Lily really been sick for this long? My mind felt overwhelmed, so I didn't bother thinking about it. I just kept moving, setting the pie down on the counter top.

The Johanssons were a very... conservative couple. Old-fashioned. They didn't believe in much except for the Christian church. I'd only met with them on a few occasions, but I knew I had to impress them this time, if I wanted any information about Mama's parents. I took a deep breath and left the pie cooling on the counter, going to check my reflection in the bathroom one last time.

A pretty girl stood before me.

Curly, dusty hair, that I'd done my best to untangle, reached almost past my ribs. I had on a nice Sunday dress, with a flowery print that I disliked the more I looked at it. It was one of my two nice dresses, and I knew I should be happy to have it because hardly any of the girls outside town had such nice clothes as these. But I still hated it.

I straightened up and folded my collar down neatly. I nodded at my reflection, swallowing hard. "You can do this," I said to myself. "You *can* do this," I stammered slightly, chewing on my lip. There was no way I could do this. But I wanted to know the truth. Sticking my nose where it didn't belong, all the time. That was me. Alex the Snoop. Then I reprimanded myself sharply. This did in fact involve me! It was my Mama this was all about. So I deserved to know something, at least.

"Hey, whatcha made me?" Somebody called from the kitchen. I looked up in panic and hustled out the door and down the hallway. Willie was just reaching for the pie with a knife.

"No!" I yelled, grabbing it away from him. I shook my head, glaring incredulously at him. He held both hands up in protest and backed away.

"Alex," he said slowly, "Put th' knife down."

I realized I was pointing the butter knife at him. I let my shoulders fall and set the knife softly on the counter. "I'm trying to do something important here, Willie," I pleaded with him.

Head tilted, eyes narrowed and mouth poised to speak, he stared at me. Then he shut his mouth and cleared his throat. Then, turning his back on me, Willie grabbed a hunk of bread off the table and began gnawing on it.

I waited anxiously, wondering what he was possibly thinking about. Apple pie wasn't something you just *made* for no reason at all. And it was made from some of our last apples. He'd think it was a waste. He'd tell Papa. He'd demand an explanation.

"There were a time when I asked you t'let me go without askin' questions." He didn't even turn around to face me. I realized where he was going with this.

"But Willie, that ended badly! You got hurt that day!"

He chuckled. "Somethin' tells me you got more sense 'n I ever did." He turned to face me again, expressionless.

"Go. I'll call them hounds if you ain't back by sunset." With that he turned away again.

So I picked up the wasteful little pie and left my home behind. The Johanssons had a sunny little cabin, with a slanted roof and a lovely deck. Two worn old wicker rocking chairs sat above the stairs, swaying in the breeze. Everything was picturesque and perfect. It was creepy. I shivered.

I wasn't even right sure how to call the Johanssons to their door. Setting the pie down for a moment, I walked up to their door and took a deep breath. Then I knocked, boldly and loudly, surprising myself. I heard floorboards creaking, so I hastily picked up my pie and readied myself. Mrs. Johansson answered the door, peering at me through thick spectacles.

"Yes?" Her voice was high and yet heavy, somehow. Grating.

"Ah, yes, ma'am, my name is Alexandria, I live not very far from here. We're neighbors."

Mrs. Johansson adjusted her glasses and leaned closer to me. Her face was a mass of wrinkles. Scant gray hair was piled atop her head in a failing bun.

She pulled back in recognition, opening the door wider. "Oh yes, I remember now. Alex. How you've grown," She said airily. "Do come in, dearie." I held the pie close to me, feeling its fading warmth through the tin.

She shuffled away from the door, calling through the house, "James! We have a visitor!" Then she turned back to me, squinting. "Is that an apple pie you've brought us? Wonderful. Hand it here, I'll cut a few slices." A trickle of anticipation tinged with anxiety passed through me. I hoped the pie would taste okay.

Mrs. Johansson bustled away into the kitchen with the pie. I took a few steps to the right into their front room. A wicker chair with a padded seat and a long brown couch sat by the red brick fireplace. I chose the chair, not wanting to sit next to anyone.

Mr. Johansson clomped into the cabin, his long, bushy eyebrows nearly hiding his eyes. He had a scraggly gray beard shot through with black and a sagging face, like an old hound dog. He peered at me, lifting his shaggy eyebrows, and then turned wordlessly into the kitchen. I waited in nervous silence, straightening the hem of my dress.

Moments later, Mr. and Mrs. Johansson both returned and sat down on the couch, each with a plate of pie. Mrs. Johansson handed me a plate. I looked at my slice of pie. It was awfully small.

With her nose lifted, Mrs. Johansson gave a tiny nod. "You, my dear, must eat small portions and grow up a proper little lady. Otherwise the boys will never look twice at you," she said primly. I noticed that her piece wasn't quite so proper. I stared in distaste at the pie, then at Mrs. J., deciding in a split second that I didn't like her very much at all.

She gave a tiny cough. "Now then, dearie, is there a reason you dropped by here or had you just come to bring us unnecessary sweets?" The words, though non-threatening, sent a chill of dislike through me. She was very old, that I could see, but not grandmotherly at all. I felt sorry for any children who might have called her that.

"Uh, no," I started, wondering at myself. I hadn't actually planned this out in my head. Did I even think I would make it this far?

I cleared my throat and tried to start again. "You see, I, I mean, my Mama–"

Mrs. Johansson cut me off scornfully. "My girl, you're a bit old to be using that word. Be a dear and use the proper word. 'Mother'. Say it now, like a lady."

A sour feeling gripped my throat and puckered my chin. "Mother." I choked out.

Mrs. Johansson nodded, satisfied. "Now continue. And be clear about it," she added. "I do hate it when young ones don't speak clearly."

Disbelief surged up in me. Who was this woman to talk down on me like this? I numbed my feelings and blinked away white-hot tears. My humiliation melted down inside me.

"I recently came across something odd concerning my... mother, and wanted to inquire about it." I quipped coldly. Mama's schooling never did fail me.

Mrs. Johansson lifted her eyebrows and leaned back, both hands crossed on her knees. She turned to look at Mr. Johansson, the skin on her neck sagging and bunching. They exchanged a glance somehow – I couldn't even tell what color the man's eyes were, they were so hidden beneath faded skin and eyebrow – then she turned back to me, eyes narrowed.

"Why exactly did you come to us to, as you put it, *inquire* about your mother?" I sat back, confused. Were they uncomfortable? Why on earth would my asking about Mama make them squirm?

"Not for any particular reason, actually. You've just lived here a long time, just like Mama–" Mrs. Johansson cleared her throat and raised one eyebrow expectantly.

I felt rage surge up in me and then mutate into cold disdain. "Oh, *do* excuse me," I said with exaggerated politeness. "I believe I meant mother." An empty feeling grew in my chest. I felt uncomfortable in my chair, like I was unable to sit properly under her assessing gaze. I just wanted to leave.

I didn't give them time to wonder if I had an attitude behind my frilly words. "Anyhow, pardon me, I came to ask you if you knew my mother's family when she was my age." Both the Johanssons stiffened. Mrs. Johansson hem-hawwed and then offered to take my dishes. I hadn't even touched the pie yet, but, deaf to my protesting, she picked up the plate and waddled to the kitchen. Mr. Johansson excused himself as he followed his shrew of a wife into the kitchen. He barely looked at me. His voice was low and gravelly, something like bone being dragged over rocks. I shuddered.

I craned my neck after the elderly couple and decided to take a look around their front room. *Surely they wouldn't mind*, I thought, snickering, and rose up quietly from my seat. I turned to my right and knew in my gut that if I were to find something, it would be there. A large, dark bookcase towered against the far wall, its shelves shadowed and inviting. Two big cabinet doors were closed at its bottom, sheltering secrets and old memories.

I went straight for the doors. The one on the left swung open easy enough, creaking loudly as it did so. I winced visibly, listening. No sound came from the kitchen, so I slid a hand inside the cubby and searched around inside. I pulled out some old papers, a yellowing old news sheet, and a bible. I replaced the items carefully and turned to the right door. Pulling on the handle, I furrowed my eyebrows in dismay. It wouldn't budge. I held my breath and pulled harder, and suddenly the door popped open loudly, cracking against the wall and then hanging loosely on its squeaking joints. Terrified that they had heard, I paused for a moment. Silence.

I set my jaw and pulled out whatever I could find. Papers, documents, a stack of photos, some more books. I stopped, my gut pulling me to the photos. I looked at them closer and started going through them quickly. A wedding. A new baby. A birthday party. A family portrait.

I dropped the pictures and held a hand over my mouth, dismayed. I fell back on one hand like I'd been punched in the gut with a brick. All the air left my lungs and mocked me as I wrestled for breath.

There, on the floor before me, was the picture of Mama and her parents.

Mama and the Johanssons.

CHAPTER NINETEEN

Every nerve in my body bristled in horror. The *Johanssons were my grandparents?!* I took a deep breath, having trouble processing. But it all made terrible sense now. Mama had obviously had some reason to leave these people – I didn't like them at all, and I'd only just properly met them.

Suddenly my skin prickled and I looked up in terror. The elderly couple, *my grandparents,* were standing in the kitchen doorway, staring. They stood like shadows of people, their eyes blankly boring into me, accusing, judging. Mortified, I scrambled up and away, leaving the pictures in a scattered mess on the floor. The one photo of Mama and the Johanssons looked up at me from my hand as I moved toward the door on stumbling feet. I grasped the door handle with clammy hands and abandoned all pretense of caution, running and slipping down the porch steps as fast as I could.

I half-slid down the wet wood, throwing my arms out for balance. I hit the ground running, headed back for my house. Terror pulsed in my veins, terror and surprise and awful numb illness in the back of my throat. I wanted to escape what I had only just found. Every time my feet hit the ground, slapping up more and more mud, I felt my pulsing heartbeat sync with them.

Mud? I stopped dead, sliding, and almost fell over. When I regained my balance, I stuck out a hand in wonder. Rain was coursing down out of the sky in a thick sheeting fog of silver.

Rain. The cold, clean water was such a change from the everyday dust of Colorado that I threw up my hands and let the life-giving torrent pour over me. It cleansed my skin and my face, wiping away all dust and hurt in its tread. I laughed, and brief, awe-filled joy danced inside me. What a beautiful thing this was, this wonder of nature. God's creation healing itself. I took a deep breath of the misty air, the fog that was rising from the hot ground. It was delicious, pouring through my body and reviving all the dusty worn-out parts of me.

I could imagine the rain seeping into the dirt, grounding the dust temporarily and restoring life to our crops. I wanted to cry, it was so beautiful and so unexpectedly sweet. Instead I laughed aloud, my cheeks flushed bright red, hands thrown out as I twirled and spun in the storm. Thunder cracked above me, rattling the sky with a tremendous roar. I shook my head with airy glee, light-headed with the crisp, clean scent of the washed ground. Eventually I collapsed to the mud, feeling the cold rain pool around me and splash down onto me. I crawled over to shelter beneath a tree, huddled in its roots, watching the storm lash its branches above me. I imagined myself a part of the tree, muddy roots gratefully exposed to the rain. *Being washed clean,* I reminded myself.

"That's how it feels when God forgives you, except on the inside," Mama said. Four-year-old Alex looked up at her with huge, adoring eyes as Mama gave her a bath. Mama splashed some water at Alex, and the little girl giggled. Mama's eyes were warm and full of love for her daughter.

"See," she said in her special voice she used to use just for baby Alex, "All clean! Just like on the inside." Smiling, she poked Alex in the tummy and then wrapped her in the warm folds of soft cloth, hugging her close.

I sat securely against the tree, arms circled around my knees as refreshing, chilly rain swept the skies around me. I held on to the bittersweet memory of Mama as long as I could. It was a flash, just a broken fragment of what I wished I could remember of Mama. All the years she'd spent with me, and I had only precious few memories of her to hold on to – and they were fading. I didn't want to admit it, didn't want to allow it, but Mama's face was growing dim in my memory. Her eyes were slowly losing sharpness in my mind, and I couldn't quite recall the shape of her smile.

I shivered against the trunk of the tree and realized I was crying into the rain. Just crying as loud as I wished, for the droplets thrumming on the ground would cover the sound of my tears, and no-one was here to listen to them anyway. Bitter sorrow was seeping out of me, like poison leaving a wound. It was being flushed out of me by the freezing cleanliness of the rain. I sat there until my tears stopped, until the fear that I would forget her was soothed. The cold surrounded me, but I felt so warm. Emptiness echoed inside me where my sorrow had been nestled, and I felt the beauty of God's storm filling the chasm with raw promise.

Finally I left the tree. My mind returned to the photo. Where had I put it? I searched my pockets, finding nothing. Guilty panic began to ease in. I whirled around and searched the ground, trying desperately to see through the foggy curtain.

I shielded my eyes against the rain. *There!* I spotted something lying forlornly beside a puddle, looking water-worn and drenched. *The photo!* With fear clawing at my throat, I grabbed it up quickly and shoved it under my shirt; then I began to run.

The rain had slackened off quite a bit, but I was still slipping and sliding everywhere in the mud as I ran. Finally I reached my home and opened the door. It swung slowly, hanging onto the frame, the old metal giving a prolonged squeal. The threshold beckoned me with new grace, offering steps I had never taken before. Clothes heavy and cold, I trudged inside.

Suddenly a huge burst of overwhelming feeling surged up inside me. Papa had been hiding this! He'd been pretending to know nothing, and that the photo meant nothing. Now he would have to tell me the entire truth!

I stopped cold as I crossed the threshold and entered the kitchen. Papa was staring down into a bowl of water with a cloth in one hand, eyes empty and lost. He looked like he'd forgotten why he was there. *What now?* I thought with pounding clarity. *What now?*

"Papa," I said slowly. "What's wrong?"

He looked up at me, and raw, angry tears surprised me from his eyes. "Deep illness done crept into her lungs. She ain't fightin' it off too well, Alex. Willie went runnin' for the doc." Papa looked down at the ground, mumbling, "Dust pneumonia. We tried so hard t'keep 'er from the dust..." I shivered. Images of Lily's spent body crowded my mind, and all I could see was the ghostly figure of disease reaching a clotting hand down into her lungs. Her twisted limbs pulsed in my memory, broken, useless, and unable to fight for life...

Papa's hands were shaking and he looked terrible. His greatest fear was to walk this earth without us.

I left Papa in a hurry, rushing to Lily's room, to her bedside, staring down at her pale face. "Lily!" I called urgently, gently shaking her shoulder. "Lily!" Color was flushed into her cheeks, to where her face looked bright red. Her eyes were shut and her mouth closed. Panic dumped into my veins, red-hot and demanding me to do something.

Desperate, I put my cheek up to Lily's face. I heard the weakest stream of air, muggy and rasping. I took deep breaths and tried to calm my racing heart. "Oh, God... I can't do this again..."

I struggled to calm myself. Memories of Mama's death were threatening to return with their accusations and guilt. *All your fault, your fault...* menacing whispers seemed to gather around me. I covered my ears and closed my eyes, sinking against the wall behind me. Terror pulsed where my heart should have been, and every lungful of air was like trying to breathe smoke. My senses were assaulted by memories. Roaring and crackling and that insistent, sibilant whisper filled my mind. Then a soft phrase took form inside me and pushed against all the darkness, all the anxiety and shadows that kept me petrified.

"This too will pass." Flashes of Mama cut through the day-mare, breaking the cold with a purifying warmth. I remembered her with us: reading the Bible to us in the darkest hours of the night; during storms; watching us carefully at the

market; speaking in her soft, confident voice that demanded everyone listen. The evil whisper clawed at me, trying to find purchase, but Mama's words flowed over me like running water and the whispering slid away. The flames in my mind sputtered out, sizzling and then dying to silence. God had given me a mama to protect me, and even now He led her memory to coax me from despair. I felt a glowing warmth that crept into my limbs and gave me will to confront this darkness.

I opened my eyes and saw nothing at first. Pure shadows. I blinked, and Lily's shallow breathing filled the air, grating on my ears. It seemed louder now; infected, broken, dying. It was the sound of sickness. I realized something. Lily was going to die. There was nothing we could do, and nowhere on this earth left to turn. Bitterly, I understood that broth would not help her now.

I took a deep breath and spoke through the shadows. "Lord, this is the end of earthly help for Lily. She can't walk any farther in this world without your help. If you want to take her home, so be it. But please, end her suffering now, whether it's by healing or her final breath. I'm asking you now," I said. I felt strength flood my bones. The Holy Spirit made its presence known. "Please finish this."

Then a single light tentatively lit in the shadows, simply existing, simply being. It glimmered and suddenly it burst forth into tremendous volumes, a light so blazingly bright that I could not bear to go on looking. I held my eyes, fearful for my sight after looking upon something fierier than the sun. The light was crowding upon me, engulfing me, catching all in its embrace, flinging the darkness away like a disgusting cloak. All felt impure in the presence of the light; the very sky seemed simplistic and inadequate, the stars mere dirty fireflies before this greater presence. Then the unbearable brilliance became softer, and a flowing radiance replaced it. I dared to look and my eyes widened in awe, drinking in the scene before me. There beside Lily, whose chest was still and her body and twisted limbs limp and lifeless, stood an angel.

I was terrified, but light poured from him, and the being rumbled peace in an eloquent greeting. I tried to take a step forward, but it was like being encased in stone. I could not move or look away; nor would I ever wish to. The angel raised a hand, beauty and perfection surrounding him whole like heavy waters. Delight poured from him, joy in his mission this night, joy in his very existence. He lifted his hand forth, toward my sister. Somehow, an even purer light flowed from his hand and slipped over Lily, engulfing her silently. It poured over her bed and covers, under them, through them, surrounding her with light so pure and sure that it looked to be solid life. Lily began to breathe, and to move slowly, and the light moved with her, soft and radiant and perfect. Her face became blurred, and slowly the rest of her faded, too. She began to melt into the light. I felt fear stirring in my chest, but the being looked right at me and an echo poured forth from him, tinged with gentle reassurance.

I stood staring in awe at him, this radiant, holy being that was clearly worthy of having been created by the Lord of all things. This was no baby with wings, as I'd seen painted in the stained glass of the church. This angel was like nothing I could imagine. My eyes and brain begged for a comparison to understand his form and the way the angel looked, but nothing on earth was equal. The angel was brimming to the top with majesty and power, power so incredible that I had no doubt of my safety in his presence.

The fear in my heart was gone. I settled and watched, not moving, not daring to draw breath.

The light encasing Lily became brighter and brighter, her form invisible within it, and tears coursed down my face because of its intensity. Then all at once, the light slipped away, dissipating silently, leaving a silky remnant of purity behind. I wondered if she was dead. No fear beleaguered me; only a strong curiosity.

The being looked at me again. Suddenly, the memory of my Mama's voice touched my ears, called out of my dreams by the appearance of one of the Lord's Heavenly servants. And I wept as I remembered her singing once again the song from my dreams, only now brought to me in the waking world. The words of the song burned into my mind, blazing with love and pride. I fell to the ground, my face a mess of tears, my eyes shut tightly with pain and healing and forgiveness.

I felt His servant leave. I felt that single essence of purity leave my presence, and wept all the harder. God had done this. God had sent a mighty warrior with a mission tonight. He had shown me with spiritual eyes this incredible scene. Forever I would carry this encounter within me. I sat on the floor beside Lily's bed, weeping. And when the tears ran out, I stood up in a daze of peace and agony. No moment more perfect had ever been.

Dimly I was aware of Papa having entered the room. I was full of a new peace, with no fear or pain left within me. The torment within me about Mama and her past was appeased. No questions rang in my mind, no burning hatred for me or my world was left. My Mama loved me. She was alright, this I knew. I felt it in the rumble of the angel's voice. I could forgive myself now, truly forgive myself. I felt so at ease, so comfortable and assured, and I knew with a certainty that could not be questioned that my sister would live.

She was healed, and she would live.

CHAPTER TWENTY

The next morning dawned swift and sunny. I yawned and sat up, stomach rumbling. Suddenly, bright wakefulness dumped into my veins like liquid sunshine – *Lily had been healed.* I shot up to my feet and ran into her room, bouncing with energy, to look at her bed.

It was empty. Joy so strong and dizzying rushed through me that I swayed and saw dark colors melt over my vision in dripping pools.

Willie, having walked in, grabbed my arm, steadying me. "Woah there, cowboy. Good mornin'."

I shook off his arm good-naturedly. "Where's Lily at?" Willie just laughed and led me into the kitchen, where a very astounded Dr. Jones was conversing with my father.

Papa.

It seemed as though ten years had simply jumped right off Papa's face. His eyes sparkled when he spoke again, his wrinkles looked like trophies instead of burdens, and his hair looked darker than ever. He was speaking and gesturing wildly to the doctor, probably describing with incredulity how happy we all were, to find the youngest of our family healed of a terrible disease.

Lily was just sitting there, eating, all normal-like. It was surreal.

Sitting at the kitchen table, stuffing in bread.

Lily, my Lily.

Awake, alive, okay.

She's okay.

All the shock and incredible emotion I'd felt earlier began to pour over me once again, flooding me with feeling. I was intoxicated with shock and joy. "Lily." I said softly.

She turned to me, and her face broke into an enormous grin. *"Alex!"*

And she jumped up and tackled me to the ground. Horrified, I began to protest, "What are you doing, you'll—" Then I realized she was fine. Whole. Restored. She was well. I could hug her without fear of bruising or cutting her fragile skin. She was *healthy* again. Light and energy radiated off of her face, seeming to fill the whole room with the beautiful glow of life.

I took a seat across from her, watching her eat freshly-baked bread. I wondered who'd made it for her. Mostly, though, I just sat with my head on my arms, gazing across the table at my little sister. She was alive.

I just sat there, staring across the table. Lily looked so much older and bigger. All that time, lying in bed, she'd looked tiny and ill and young. Now, restored to life as it should have been, I was aware of how much she'd grown and the way her face had matured. My little sister was healed. The words echoed in my mind with an absolute finality and the beautiful promise of a long life yet for her to live.

She's healed.

God had done an incredible thing, and I was ecstatic to share it with everyone. Lily's life had just begun anew, and she could do incredible things with the path God had prepared for her. Willie joined us at the table, sitting across from Lily and next to me. We exchanged an immensely over-emotional glance. Surprise, awe, wonder, joy, and fear passed between us. We had been witness to something amazing this day.

I saw the doctor turn to Willie and ask him something. Willie laughed and shrugged, knocking on his own chest with one fist. The doctor smiled and turned back to Papa.

I glanced over at Papa, wondering when Doc Jones would leave... *because obviously, Lily was fine.* I felt elation rush through me as I said those words in my head. What a victory it was, just to be able to say those words.

The doctor was gripping his hat with a white-knuckled hand. His face said joy but his eyes cried disbelief. If he hadn't seen the miracle before and after for himself, he probably wouldn't have believed it. Then Papa walked him to the door and he was gone, walking hurriedly down the path. Papa sank down into a kitchen chair next to Lily. He looked at her, shaking his head slowly.

With a huge sigh, he collapsed over the table, mumbling, "It's over. She made it." Then he leaped to his feet and pulled us, all three of us, with him, and he pushed our hands toward the sky, laughing in jubilation and victory.

"She made it!"

The next day passed in a happy blur. Lily wanted to eat *everything* – I do mean everything – but the doctor insisted on a diet of bread and broth for the first day, simply because she hadn't eaten anything in so long. Dr. Jones didn't seem to understand that Lily was *healed*. That meant *all better*. No longer sick. *Healthy*.

I knew she was healed, and not just by the way she crammed in the food! I had to bring out two extra loaves of bread that night. Lily was an unceasing bundle of joy. Bouncing off the walls, helping with the chores, singing, running, dancing.

Willie reflected all of her happiness. I could see it in his eyes every time she went whirling by. He'd watch her go, then turn and laugh with me.

Lily would run up to me, tugging at me, "Alex! Alex! Guess what!" And I would turn and ask her what.

Then she'd beam at me, her eyes crinkling, and cackle, "This doesn't hurt!" And she'd clap her hands and do a cartwheel and jostle and jump around. And I'd feel joy so sharp it almost hurt. In fact it did hurt sometimes, seeing her so happy, because it forced me to remember that so much of her childhood had been stolen from her. Of course, all it took was a second of hearing her laughter, and all that pain was eased.

Lily was so tired from her first day of freedom that she slept in 'til 10 the next morning. I kept waking in the night, going to her bedside to check on her. This time the silence didn't frighten me.

Willie and I awoke long before Lily did. We decided to make a bunch of pancakes. Willie knew how to make stew – I'd shown him a long time ago – but come breakfast time, he was almost useless. I had to show him how to do everything.

I turned to tell him that we should get out the fancy syrup from the store for our pancakes and stopped midsentence. He was already taking it out of the cupboard. I pulled a face. That had been happening a lot. We were spending far too much time together.

"Get outta my head, Willard," I said in a reedy voice.

Willie rolled his head around on his shoulders and wiggled his fingers. "I'm one o'them fortune tellers, all up in yer mind," he said. "Watch out or I'll turn youse inter a frog." He tip-toed over and pulled at my ponytail, making whooshing noises which I assumed he thought sounded magical.

I tried to pull free. "Owch! Stoppit!" I swung an arm at him.

Cackling, he sidestepped me and headed off toward the front room, calling back, "Shhhh!! If we're too loud, Lily's goin' wake up!"

I stared after him in bewilderment. He was so weird. But he *was* my best friend. I shook my head and stretched to grab a dish from the cupboard. I needed a mixing bowl. I was gonna make some pancakes, eggs, and bacon for Lily. We also had that syrup from town!

We'd had to trade a couple jars of our preserved berries for the syrup, but it was worth it. I felt really excited to set this food out for Lily. She was going to love the breakfast. Papa was working with the crops right now, what was left of them. It was great of him just to allow me and Willie this day to spend with Lily. He told us to do as we wished for breakfast and then take her somewhere for the day. She hadn't left the house in so long. I had thought long and hard about where I wanted to take her, and Willie and I stayed up half the night whispering about it. We'd finally decided on a perfect place.

I smiled to myself just thinking about it. Lily was going to have the best day today. It was so surreal – so *amazing* – one moment she was dying... The next, she was healed.

I'd stayed awake in bed for what felt like forever the night before, thanking God. Just in a daze, thanking him for everything that he'd done. It was so beyond amazing. It was beyond my comprehension in every way. I would never be able to fathom it. I decided then and there to try and bring this joy to everyone I met. I wanted other people to be saved, too. It hurt my soul to imagine anyone missing out on God's grace. It hurt so much that I couldn't breathe, so I tried not to focus on lost souls. I tried to focus on Lily and everything that had happened to us. My family had been through a lot in a few short months.

I yanked myself back to the present. The bacon was sizzling in a pan on the stove and my pancakes were steaming on a plate on the counter. Now I just needed to fry the eggs. Actually...

"Hey, Willie," I called. He trotted into the kitchen.

"Yeah?"

I handed him the handle of the bacon pan. "Here, finish this. It's almost done. When you're finished with that, take those eggs..." I gestured at the bowl of freshly gathered eggs on the table, "...and fry 'em up. Well done, scrambled," I instructed. That was how Lily liked eggs. I preferred over easy, but this was about her.

It was nearing 8:00 now. We didn't know how long Lily would sleep. Chills swept through me every time I realized all over again that Lily wasn't sick anymore. I spent the whole morning grinning like a sap, overwhelmingly happy with my task.

"Hey," said Willie, jostling me. "Hey, how do I rightly know if these is done?" He was shaking the bacon around in the pan, trying to keep it from burning. I laughed.

"They're done," I said, smilingly shaking my head as I removed the pan from the burner and dumped the bacon out onto a plate. It lay there, sizzling. I sniffed appreciatively. "This all smells incredible," I sighed.

Willie wasn't listening. He was squinting down at the pan as he cracked eggs into it, tongue stuck out in concentration. His face resembled Papa's when he was trying to braid my hair.

I rolled my eyes and moved all the food to the table. Finished with my task, I turned to Willie confidently. "Eggs done?" I said, standing on tip-toe, trying to see into the pan around him.

"Just about," he replied, glancing back at me.

I crossed the kitchen. "We're pretty much done here, then."

Turning to look at the eggs, I blinked in surprise. They looked perfect! "Willie, you aren't half bad at cooking," I said, in shock.

He raised his nose at me primly. "I got lots o' hidden talents," he said, "in afact, I'm also a purdy dancer." With that, he left the eggs to me and twirled away toward Lily's room to see if she was awake yet. Willie looked so down right odd, waving his arms about and prancing on tip-toes, his curly hair bouncing; I had to check my laughter, trying not to let Willie know that he was funny as well as a "purdy" dancer. He was too good at making himself look foolish. I went back to my food, rushing to make sure everything was set.

Hastily I set out dishes for us all to use, and some forks and knives. Then I myself sat, with empty seats around me, waiting for Lily and Willie. We had already set aside some of the food for Papa. He could eat it later.

"C'mon, lazybones," came Willie's voice down the hallway. He appeared around the corner, dragging Lily along by her arm. She was rubbing her eyes with her free hand, her hair askew, looking quite the little monster. I laughed, and Lily looked up. Her face went from sleepy to hungry in half a moment, and she bounded over, all drowsiness forgotten completely.

"Pancakes? *Syrup*? From the store?" She asked, and I could hear the hunger in her voice. Willie came strolling in and sat next to me.

"That's right, but it ain't for you," he said, winking at me.

I pulled a proper face. "This kind of food is for Prince Willard and I, Princess Alexandria," I said, struggling not to laugh.

Lily looked from me to Willie and back again, unsubdued. "Your real name is Willard?" Then, in one swift movement, she plopped down and filled her plate with bacon, eggs and pancakes, digging in with a will. Willie and I looked at each other and then burst out laughing.

Lily was back and better than ever.

We ate jovially that morning, fully enjoying the wonderful cooking and heart-happy atmosphere. Then Willie and I sent Lily "on a mission" to pick flowers out back of the barn.

After she'd scampered off, I turned to my friend, wondering, "Are there even any flowers growing out there?"

Willie shrugged and said, "We needed time, right? So," he added, "ain't no flowers, ain't no rush." He winked.

I just snorted. "You're terrible." Then we began to pack a basket full of food, readying ourselves to take Lily on a picnic by the creek-fed pond a mile or two west of our land. It was a beautiful place – we'd gone there several times as a family, with Mama and Papa. Our parents would sit in the shade while we went off to explore and play, often falling in the pond. It didn't matter, though, because we both knew how to swim. It was a rare place in the dry atmosphere of southeastern Colorado, and I figured it'd be plenty alive after the huge storm we'd had not too many days ago.

A thick outcropping of trees surrounded the pond, too, giving shelter and shadow to plenty of creatures. It was a beautiful place that Lily knew well, and she would be delighted to spend the day there with her sister and brother.

I loved my family and my life. Times were getting tougher, indeed, but nothing is impossible with the Almighty on your side.

CHAPTER TWENTY-ONE

Standing up, I examined the basket. Inside was plenty of food for lunch. It didn't seem very appetizing right now, but after our lengthy trek it would be well-appreciated. Lily came trailing in with a fistful of weedy flowers. She dropped 'em on the counter, brushing the dirt from her hands. I winced.

Lily peered at the basket. "We goin' somewhere?" She said questioningly.

Feeling confused, I answered, "Well, yeah. We got a special day planned."

Lily pondered the ground for a moment and then said, "We ain't gotta work today?"

I looked at her, feeling disbelief knead me from inside, and I shook my head slowly. "No, Lil. No work for you, not yet. Times ain't that tough. God wouldn't have healed you just to work you to the bone right off," I said, grinning. Lily winked at me and grabbed my hand. Then she outstretched her other hand to Willie, who looked at it with raised eyebrows and then took it. She dragged us roughly to the door, just leavin' me time to grab the basket as we swept past. Willie remarked, "Lil Monster, we ain't gonna fit out the door three wide."

Lily let go of our hands and flounced out the door. "Fine! I'll go by myself," She laughed.

I looked exasperatedly at Willie. "See what you did? Now she thinks she's all grown up and such nonsense," I said matter-of-factly. Willie snorted at me and ran after Lily, yelling, "I'm gonna getcha!" She yelped and dashed away from him. I was about to check their behavior when I relaxed. Why would I restrict their joy? I didn't have to protect Lily anymore. She was safe. And Willie was steering Lily in the right direction. In fact...

"Wait for me!" I cried, catching up to Willie. "We can corner her!" We glanced at each other and ran a bit faster, surprised at Lily's speed. Lily was laughing so hard she could hardly breathe, stumbling through the dust with her deep brown hair swingin' about. Despite the healing, she had a lot of hair to grow back. The sickness had thinned it out considerably.

But that didn't matter a trifle, because she was healthy and happy, and if anything, her hair was a reminder of what she had overcome. I smiled to myself. What *we* had overcome. I sent another silent prayer to God, thanking him all over again for watching over us. Despite anything I may ever think, despite my anger and my rage at him sometimes for letting Mama go away, I knew he would always work all things for my good. I sighed deeply, just enjoying the knowledge that as long as I listened to Him, I'd be alright.

I didn't have to worry or be anxious or afraid, even though I couldn't help feeling those things sometimes. My Father had everything in control. This world was senseless and violent and full of turmoil – which was why I was so, so eternally grateful to have a guiding light. A savior, a messiah, the love of my life – I never had to be afraid. Even if I couldn't always feel it, there was always hope.

"Aleeex," wailed Lily. I snapped back to the present. We'd been walking for roughly an hour and a half. Any doubts that I could have about Lily's strength were gone. She'd been ahead of us nearly the entire time. It was Willie and I having trouble keeping up!

"Yeah, Lily?" I responded.

She looked up at me with giant dark eyes. "Soooo… Where are we going?" She skipped through the dirt, scuffing it with her shoes.

I feigned being taken aback. "Woahh, you're not gonna ask 'how much longer' or 'when do we eat' like usual?" I teased her. She shook her head and said, "No, I'm a good kid. The best. Best sister ever," She beamed at me. I laughed.

"Not gonna work, Lil," I replied, and her eyes narrowed. Little trickster.

Then she resorted to begging. "Pleeeease, please tell me where we're goin'!" She was desperate, yes, but the huge smile on her face denied any upset. She was too happy to be here to actually be bothered about our destination, so I refused to tell her.

I pursed my lips and played the silent game, like they taught us in school, and Lily turned to throw herself on Willie. "Wiiiilllliiieeee," she wailed. "Alex won't tell me where we're goin'!"

He made a horrified face. "She won't? How dare she!" Then he winked at me. I huffed.

Lily waited expectantly, looking at Willie pointedly as we walked. He whistled a tune for a while and then looked over at her. "Oh! Did you want somethin'?" He asked innocently.

Lily punched him on the arm. "Yeeees, tell me where we're goin'!"

Willie stopped, and we stopped with him. He stroked his chin and looked out across the land, back at the lumpy shape of the town.

Then he looked at Lily and said slowly, "You're right, I reckon. I prob'ly should tell you." She nodded eagerly. "One problem, though," Willie said, as he began to walk again. We kept pace with him.

Lily waited. "What problem?"

Willie chuckled and threw his hands up in the air. "She didn't tell me neither!" I shook my head at his deception.

Lily gasped and stomped in mock frustration. "Then we're just gonna have to get there faster!" I exchanged an exhausted glance with Willie, and then we took off after her.

"She sure is... lively when... she's alive," Willie panted. I laughed. It was like some sort of delightful joke. She was alive and well. I felt myself grinning widely.

"Pretty odd, huh? We've... gotten out of shape... since she's been under," I answered between breaths as we ran.

Willie laughed and cried, "Oh, yeah, how nice that were!" Our shoulders shook as we laughed and we had to stop, wheezing.

"Lily, come back here now. We're almost there," I called to her. She turned around, only about a dozen feet ahead, and ran back obediently.

"We are? We are? We are?" She spewed, jumping up and down on the balls of her feet.

"Woah, yes, yes, down, child!" I laughed.

Lily ran in a quick, tight circle, bursting with energy even after the few-mile walk. *She must be feeling amazing,* I thought to myself. It was true. After being all twisted up for so long, such complete and sudden freedom would be indescribable.

I pointed to a clump of trees ahead. "Recognize that place, Lil?"

Lily tilted her head sideways, gazing at it through slanted eyes. Then a jolt of recognition shot through her eyes, and she turned to me to affirm her memory.

"That's where we went with Mama?"

I just smiled at Lily. "That's the place."

As we walked in through the trees, I narrowed my eyes, searching. Finding the pond would be easier once we located the creek. After walking for ten minutes with no sign of it, I began to feel confused. Surely it wasn't gone? Suddenly I stumbled into a low ditch with some muddy water at the bottom, catching myself on tiptoe and fingertips.

"Woah," called Willie as he and Lily peered down at me.

I looked around. "I think I found the creek," I said. The water had lowered so much in the drought that the little riverlet was nearly dry. But following the carved earth downhill through the trees, we managed to come upon the remains of the pond. It had shrunk considerably. I tried not to let it, but a lingering doubt began to grasp my heart. This could really let Lily down. It seemed like it could be a sign, ominous and chock-full of bad feeling.

But then I turned to look at Lily, and she was skipping rocks into the water with Willie. Trying to, anyway. The pebbles just hit the water and sank, but the two were laughing and competing anyhow. It chased away all the sudden fear inside me, and I smiled, my heart lightened once again.

We spent a long time in the shade of the trees, laughing, playing in the cool muddy water, and chasing one another through the branches of the trees. We had a contest to see who could climb the highest. Lily and I had been climbing trees for a long time, though. Willie clearly stood no chance.

He had just made it into one of the lower branches, a long, sturdy one, when suddenly he vanished with a splash. I craned my neck around the branch I was clinging to quickly.

"Willie?" The only response was silence. He'd fallen off the branch into the pond. We scrambled quickly down, calling after him, "Willie! Y'okay?"

Suddenly he popped up on the edge of the pond and yanked us both in with him! Lily screeched and I screamed as we tumbled into the murky water. The mud was cold and actually felt pretty good. Lily and I ganged up on Willie, splashing water at him and kicking up mud.

Mentally I shook my head – I was going to have to do this laundry later – but I just didn't care. These moments were priceless in every way, and I'd do thousands of basins of laundry if it meant I'd get to live this way forever.

Finally we got out of the pond and lay drying in a patch of sunlight on the bank. The shafts of sun fell just right through the twigged mats above us, picking their way through the maze of branches to slip perfectly by and warm our chilled skin.

After we dried off a bit, we sat up and got out the picnic food. I'd packed a big, fresh loaf of bread, a hunk of cheese, some red apples from the market, and a jug of water. There was no better supper for three children basking by a pond on such an afternoon.

We ate quietly, savoring the beauty of the surrounding woodland and its rarity. Lily was like a chipmunk, watching everything, her head swiveling quickly around to take it all in. She hadn't seen nature like this in... in years. Our food began to dwindle – we'd gone through it quickly – and I could tell Lily was itching to go explore. She'd be plenty safe as long as she didn't go far.

"Lily," I said slowly. "You remember our rule?"

"Yes," she quipped, twitching. "If I can't hear the sound of your voice, to come right back is my only choice," She recited quickly, ready to take off.

"Alright..." I paused. "Ready... Go!" She was up and running into the trees before I'd half got the words out. Willie and I laughed on the bank, happy to be out and doin' nothing. We sat in silence awhile, just thinking about all that had happened. Now that the world was quiet, it seemed to be all the louder. Then Willie turned to me.

"Alex," He said awkwardly. "I been thinkin' a lot lately, and there's somethin' you should know." I tensed up immediately, sensing the gravity in his voice. How could something be happening *again?* Already?

"Yeah, Willie?" I said slowly. "What's that?"

He took a deep breath and shuffled his feet in the mud near the pond's edge. "Look, I just, you all talk about God and such a lot," he said.

I stared at him. "Right...?"

He shrugged. "I just wanted you to know that..." He spoke suddenly fast, and steely, "that I don't believe right like you do! God couldn't be healin' somebody one minute, an', an' killin' somebody the next!" I gaped at him. What did he mean?

"Look, Alex," he said angrily, "it just don't make sense none." Then his shoulders sagged and he put his hands to his face, tears welling up hot in his eyes. "God just don't love me, I s'pose." And his voice was broken. I could hear it in that broken voice; he really felt unloved.

I felt sick. "Willie,' I said desperately. "Why do you think that? That God... that God doesn't love you?"

He looked at me with such cold, soul-sick eyes that I shivered. "He took Pa away, and I never got t'meet Ma. He loves you all, that's why He fixed Lily up. Who wouldn't love 'er?" He mumbled.

Willie raised his head and looked at me with those honey eyes, now full of pain and upset. "Look at me," he said angrily, gesturing at his face and hair. "God wanted them kids to hate me. So he made me like this. Made me all wrong," he was looking at the ground again, resting his arms on his knees. Tears fell down his face.

I felt a crystal heart breaking inside me, shattering and piercing my insides with shards.

"Oh, Willie," I said quietly. "How could you think that you're made wrong." It wasn't even a question – my thoughts were just spilling out of my shocked mouth. I sighed.

Willie was gazing out into the water, his eyes shadowed. Normally his sunny attributes should make it hard for him to look sad, but boy, right then did he look down. Every line in his anatomy seemed to cry out "pain". The way his mouth curved, like he was holdin' the whole world's pain inside him. The way he held his fists, clenched with white knuckles. How his eyebrows were drawn over his eyes, hooding them. Every detail spoke of Willie's sorrow.

I didn't even know what to say. How could I make this broken boy understand that God did love him? That the creator of our universe was infinite in grace and affection? All I could do was to be there for him.

"Listen, Willie," I said softly. "You need to understand something." He glanced at me, and I thought he would protest for a moment, but the emptiness in his eyes convinced me otherwise. "You can't understand God." I said firmly. "Heck, us trying to know why God lets certain things happens and intervenes other times would be like one of my ears of corn telling me how to shuck it!" Willie chuckled half-heartedly, and I felt hope prick my heart.

But then he shrugged and said, "Why does God make anythin' bad happen at all?"

"Willie," I spoke sharply at him, "let's get something straight. I don't believe God *makes* bad things happen, not evil. God heals, and protects, and sometimes He *allows*, and sometimes He nudges us back on course, maybe with a warning. But He ain't a faceless God who kills and hurts and judges without reason, whenever the fancy takes Him. He ain't a kid with a magnifying glass, burning ants on the ground."

Willie narrowed his eyes in thought. "If God don't make all that bad stuff happen, why does it, then?"

I took a deep breath, looking at him clearly and boldly. I remembered Mama explaining all of this to me. "Willie, God gave us all something called 'free will'. It means that He loves us so much, He lets us choose what we want in every situation. God wants us to ultimately choose him, and what's right in the world, but he also wants every other decision to be ours to make. He doesn't make me go to church, I go 'cause I like it.

God didn't make Mama marry my papa." Willie watched steadily as I talked, blinking slowly every now and again.

"The problem is, people do bad things with that free will. They make ugly choices. Darkness escaped into the world when the first ugly choice was made, a right long time ago."

"He never gave Lily that illness – she caught it 'cause our world is fallen and evil things exist here. Sickness and death were two of the things that came about when we chose sin over God."

Willie leaned back and took a huge breath. "So, wait," he said. "Youse tellin' me that God lets bad things happen just 'cause he wants us to be able to pick him, or somethin'? That's dumb!" He cried angrily. "That don't make sense none! Why don't he just force everybody to be good, then nobody would suffer!"

"Willie, wait…" I protested, but we both shut up as Lily came running back through the trees.

"Alex, Willie!" She called. "Look what I found!" Cupped in her hands was a tiny baby… something. I couldn't quite tell, but it looked like a rat.

"Lily, what is that," I cried in disgust. I had only glanced quickly at it. Its eyes were tightly shut, and it had a long tail with a slight curl to it. The little creature looked stunned, hunched over in her hand, terrified.

"My baby," she said proudly. "His name is Ralph."

"Lily, that better not be a rat," I stated.

She looked hurt. "Ralph isn't a rat, he's a squirrel," Lily pouted. I peered closer at it. The thing had reddish fur sprouting down the tail in a straight line, flanked by gray fur that covered the rest of its tail and its body. The paws looked too big for its little body. Looking closer, I noticed his right ear had a tear in it, bleeding sluggishly. Fleetingly I wondered if the tiny thing would survive, then I slowly began to nod at Lily. It wasn't a rat.

"Alright, it does look right enough like a squirrel. But where did you steal it from?" I exclaimed.

Lily stared at me like I'd sprouted antlers. "Steal!" She said indignantly. "I saved him!"

I raised my eyebrows and exchanged a glance with Willie, our talk forgotten for now. "Saved him? From what?"

Lily snorted dramatically. "From death!"

I stifled a chuckle. "Yes, obviously, but specifically what kind of death?"

Lily looked upset. "A cat was carrying away Ralph's siblings to eat them," She said tenderly, "and I picked him up before it got to him."

I dipped my head. "...right. What were Ralph and his siblings doing on the ground?"

She shrugged. "I dunno. Their nest was all torn up and stuff. Maybe the cat did it."

"Huh," I said, satisfied. "Well, what are we supposed to do with Ralph now?"

Lily rocked on her toes with the tiny squirrel in her palm, pleading with me. "I can keep him and take care of him and everything! Pleaaase!"

I hesitated. The squirrel looked past nursing age – so I seriously considered it for a moment. Then I remembered Mama's lessons on wild animals. Look, but don't touch, she'd always said.

"Now Lily, hold on just a moment. Let's think about this." Lily watched my face. "Ralph is pretty adorable now," I admitted, "but what about when he's older? He's going to change a lot," I said, urging her to understand. "When Ralph is full-grown, he's gonna want a whole forest of trees to run and climb in. He's a squirrel," I said gently, "not a dog." "And instead of all this," I added, waving an arm at the scene around me, "he'll have a little cage or a crate."

Lily hesitated, looking down at Ralph with eyes full of longing. The baby was cowering in her palms, seeming cold and scared. "We can't just leave him, can we? All alone?"

I thought for a moment and responded, "Lily, it's not right to take him. Especially when we know it's not where he's supposed to be." A light flicked on in Lily's eyes.

"Lil Monster," said Willie gently. "Gimme Ralph. I'll make sure he gets along alright." Lily hesitated for a moment, looking from the baby squirrel to Willie and back again.

"I want him to be... free. Not just when he's older, but all the time." I watched her with pondering eyes. "So... I'll be praying for you, Ralph..." She dropped him softly into Willie's hands, reluctantly watching Willie walk into the woods. Then she turned to me and sniffled.

I nodded encouragingly, not wanting her to get upset. "Willie will make sure Ralph is just fine."

Inwardly I was hoping that Willie was being careful. If that squirrel decided to bite Willie, it could cause some weird illness. After a few moments, Willie came walking back alone.

Lily ran up to him. "Where did you take him? Is he okay?"

Willie nodded and shushed her, saying, "He's fine, he's fine. I found 'im a new squirrel family that done took 'im in." He glanced at me as he said that, willing me not to say anything. I wasn't about to blow our cover.

"Come on, let's gather up our things and head home. The sun's going to set in a few hours," I added. We really did need to be heading back. It was a long walk, and we were all tired.

CHAPTER TWENTY-TWO

During our lengthy trek back to the house, Lily chattered nonstop about Ralph and how she was certain he loved his new family. At some point, I dropped back and asked Willie what he'd done with the squirrel.

"I left it in the hole o' some tree," he answered. "Somethin' will more'n likely make a meal outta it." He shrugged regretfully.

As we walked, my mind wandered. Nervously I asked myself when I'd talk to Papa about the Johanssons, or the secrets that surrounded both our families. My stomach churned thinkin' about it, but I knew it had to be done... What would Papa say when I revealed that I knew the truth?

Then again, it was possible that I only knew part of the truth. Mama had left those people for some reason, and I wasn't quite sure what it was. Maybe they were just horrid. I'd sensed that much in my single visit to their cabin.

I noticed Willie looking sideways at me. "What?" I asked indignantly.

"Oh, nothing," He said, waving his arms disarmingly. "Yer just funny-lookin' with your thinking face on." He grinned.

"Excuse me!" I yelped. "At least I have a thinking face! You never do any thinking!"

Lily ran back to us and jumped on Willie's back. He *oof'ed*. "Piggy back ride!" Cried Lily triumphantly.

Willie grunted, "I never said y'could break me," as he began shuffling faster along.

Lily whooped. "Faster!"

Willie rolled his eyes at me, unable to resist grinning, and began galloping along, bouncing Lily up and down as he went. I grew tired just watching them. Suddenly Willie stiffened and stopped, gasping. He let Lily down rather roughly and clutched a hand to himself, kneading his chest. I ran up to him.

"Willie, are you alright?" I asked, concern ripping at my heart. He straightened suddenly, face pale. Blood began to rush back to his face.

"Yeah, I'm fine," he said stiffly, breath uneven.

I furrowed my eyebrows, putting a hand to my hip. "Willie, what was that?" He was breathing more normally now, and the constriction in my heart loosened a bit.

"I'm fine, honest," he answered, waving me off. "I jus' git dizzy in the head every now an' agin. Pa used to say it was bad blood or some such nonsense."

I looked suspiciously at him. That hadn't looked very much like any regular dizzy spell. Then again, what did I know? He seemed fine now. With a whoop, Willie took off after Lily, and she ran giggling from him, kicking up dust. I smiled. My family was good.

My inquirin's about my grandparents slipped from my mind that night. We didn't wanna let go of our special day, but sleepiness prevailed; Willie, Lily and I all ended up snorin' early. Papa had left to do some trading after he'd worked the fields, and he didn't get back until real late. I didn't even see him that night. I remembered hoping that he'd gotten his leftovers from breakfast.

The next morning, we all decided to get back to work. Papa was sitting at the kitchen table with a cup of coffee, exhausted and lookin' worn down but happy. Willie was sitting next to him, eating some oatmeal. I didn't know or particularly care who had made it – I was just glad it was there for the taking. Hungrily I scooped a bowlful out and joined my family at the table.

"Mornin', Papa, Willie," I yawned. Willie returned the greeting. Papa just nodded at me, his eyelids droopy and swollen.

"Lily up yet?" I heard feet behind me.

"I'm right here," said Lily fuzzily, her frowzy hair all messy and tangled.

"Get some breakfast," I instructed her, trying to smooth some of her hair as she passed. She slithered away from me.

I tried to make eye contact with my father. "Papa, I got somethin' to say t'you while we work today," He mumbled something that sounded like, "'Course y'do," And went back to sipping his coffee. His big, rough hands nearly overlapped, wrapping around his mug.

Papa looked up at Willie. "Y'can weed the corn fields today, son. What's left of 'em, anyhow," He said.

There weren't too many corn stalks still alive, so weeding them should be a one-person job just fine. I was glad, cuz I wanted to talk to Papa alone. Things needed to start making sense around here. Lily trotted over with her bowl and sat in between Willie and me.

"I can do housework today," volunteered Lily.

I nodded at her. "Yes you can. Vacation's over, missy!" She chuckled at the absurdity of the idea; Polio, a vacation.

Papa finally finished his coffee and stood decisively. He was dressed for the fields already, as was I. I shoveled down the rest of my oatmeal and took both our bowls to the basin. Lily would wash them later.

Willie dawdled, so I poked him in the gut with one sharp finger. "Aren't you getting a bit big in the middle to be having seconds, porkie?" I said. It wasn't true at all. Willie was stick-thin like most kids his age.

He frowned down at his stomach and then turned the disapproving expression to me, lowering his eyebrows. His expression cleared suddenly and he waved airily.

"Whatever you say, tubbyguts," he responded dramatically. I just rolled my eyes, again, and walked away. Papa was already outside and headed for the fields. I followed him out and started to make my way to the potato crop. We needed to weed them, and it would take two realistically because it was a bigger crop than the corn. The remnants of each, anyhow.

But I was just glad to have an excuse to catch Papa by himself. I needed everything cleared up. No more secrets. I had grabbed the dried-out photo that morning and stuffed it into my pocket. It was slightly damaged from the rain; some of the grays and blacks ran together a bit, and those areas were faded and warped, but it didn't matter much. Papa would know what it was when he saw it, simple as that.

So I followed him, and we kneeled in the dust and began yanking out weeds with our bare hands. No gloves, no shovels. I braced myself to confront Papa. This wasn't going to be easy, and it'd probably gray his hair, but it would be worthwhile. I'd tried not to admit it to myself, but it actually hurt quite a bit that Mama had hidden something so big from us. I needed to know that she had a good reason, otherwise it would hurt to remember her, forever.

And I couldn't stand that. So I stood slowly and took out the photo.

Papa glanced over at me. "Alex? Why'd you stop pullin'?"

I swallowed. "Papa, I need you to look at this." He stood slowly, bewildered curiosity stamped on his face, and made his way over to me. I handed him the photograph.

His face paled. "Where'd ya... No, ne'ermind it all. Ain't nothin' but a picture," he said passively. "What of it?"

Frustration threatened to overwhelm me. "Please, Papa, I need the truth. That's Mama and her parents!"

Papa nodded slowly. "Yeah, I reckon t'is. What meanin' has it, though?" And that was when I got to it.

"Those are the Johanssons, and that's their son, Rick, Mama's brother. And she went to stay with them when he died, cause he was her brother," I realized aloud. *I really haven't put much thought into this 'til now,* I mused.

Papa stared off into the distance for a long while, and then he sighed and rubbed his eyebrows. Arms across his knees, he plopped down in the dust to sit.

"No," I said. "let's keep working. Can't we?" It would be easier that way. Papa looked at me for a moment and then shrugged. We kept working.

"So go on with your explanation," I reminded him. "Tell me why you kept our grandparents a secret."

As we kneeled and bent and dug, Papa took a deep breath. "Your mama'd been havin' feuds with them people since long afore I met her," stated Papa. I nodded to myself. So she had never gotten along with them, then. It made sense.

"She lived with 'er parents 'cross the oceans, they was Europeans. They led a right soft life. But soon as your mama was old 'nuff, she lit out on a ship for America and travelled all the way down 'ere with 'er brother, Rick. They was close."

I pondered this for a moment. Mama had lost her brother... would that be like losing Willie? A nasty ping went through me and I shook my head at the thought. I never wanted to consider losing Willie. Now that Lily was better, I didn't have to worry about her, either.

I shook myself from my self-inflicted anxiety and prompted my father. "Keep going, Papa."

He continued. "Then I met yer Mama, and y'know the rest o' that tale." He sighed. I waited for him to pick the narrative back up.

"Well afore too long, we got hitched and came 'pon the good fortune to buy this home at a half-decent price. The owner was leavin' for the city and didn't want his house or his land no more. We was real excited to find such a place for the likes o' us." He fell silent, lost in memories. I nudged him.

"Oh, yeah, right. Well, that was where yer ma's folks came in. Y'see, Alex, they gots lots o' money t' throw 'round.

That awful old couple moved allaway here from Europe, next door, just to spite your mama. And did it work." He gave a low whistle. "Mama forbade them to speak to you or even s'much as look at you. She really was fierce o'er you, and that was afore Lily were even born."

I digested the information. Mama's parents were really *that* horrible? They'd wasted a bunch of money to move overseas to a place they didn't care for, just to show their daughter that she could never be free?

Papa was looking at me, paused from his work. "How you takin' this?" He squinted at me.

I sighed. "Just fine, Papa. I sort of understand why Mama left'em in the first place. That's where I got the photo," I added. "I met them." Papa's face was shocked. Then he shook his head and continued.

"Well, when they first moved over a ways, next t'us, that was when we wanted t' leave. But we couldn't. Our lives was here, not to mention we didn't have no money to just up and move. So we ignored them, and the secret went away and got buried."

I was nodding now. "They sound bad, Papa."

Papa snorted. "They are. Did y'know, they showed up for one Thanksgivin' and wouldn't leave – and we ain't invited them in the first place – and they sat round in our front room insultin' our home and 'lack of femaleish touch'. They certainly loved that one, insultin' and degradin' your mama. T'was one of their favorite things. Oh, Alex, ain't right," he said, agitated.

"They was awful t'her. And..." Papa hesitated. I looked up instantly, half full of concern, half full of curiosity.

"What is it, Papa?" I echoed quietly, hoping he would answer me straight.

Papa gave a sad smile. "They never came to your mama's funeral. Her brother would've, if he'd been livin'."

Suddenly it all hit me and I sat down hard in the dust. I used to have an uncle – didn't have, *used* to have. He had died long ago. But the man was alive within my lifetime! I *could* have known him, if my parents hadn't hidden Mama's life from me! Upset boiled inside me, disbelief.

"Why was Rick staying with the Johanssons when he died, Papa?" I asked.

"When his folks moved out here, and your Mama 'nd me was married, Rick was sorta involved in the middle o' everythin'. It began to get ridiculous, so he finally just moved into their cabin an' settled there. He didn't want a part o' no family feud, just wanted to be part of the family. Nice enough fella."

I nodded ever so slowly. I didn't really see why Mama would remove herself from her parents. What had they done that was so horrible? I frowned to myself. There was something else bothering me. Why hadn't Papa ever decided to tell us the truth? It had been years since all that. Lily and I were older now.

"Papa, why did you hide it from us after Mama went away?" He looked at me sadly, and I felt pulsing sorrow spreading out from him in waves.

"Oh, Alex, ain't that clear," he said softly. "Ain't that the clearest o' all of it?"

I stared at him, confused. What was one possible, reasonable explanation for him hiding something like that from us? I couldn't think of a thing.

"No, Papa, I don't know. Please help me."

Papa took a ragged sigh and opened his mouth to speak once more. "I loved yer mama, always will. And when she decided to keep this secret from our kids, I supported 'er. She was protectin' you two, even afore you was born. See, Mama put up with all that roughness and bad manners from them for a long time, livin' next to us. But when she found out she was gonna have you, she ended it. Said she couldn't have them disrespectin' her with you 'round or have them maybe hurtin' you. But a secret like that, it has bad feelin', see. I couldn't have you girls rememberin' your Mama like that, don't y'unnerstan!" Papa's voice was shaking. Obviously he'd had a lot of sleepless nights over this secret.

"I would never think badly of Mama," I said softly. "Never. She was everything to me."

Papa smiled. "Everythin' but the Lord in Heaven, yes indeed. She was like that to ev'ryone."

Papa was gazing off again, stumbling through sunny pastures, lost amid the memories of his mind. I didn't want to disturb him, but I had one last thing to say. "Papa?"

"Yeah, Alex?"

My voice was dark and afraid. "I know this is a terrible idea, but... we have to go see the Johanssons."

Papa studied me. "The Johanssons? Alex, they ain't part o' our lives. Ain't now, ain't ever," he protested. I could feel the dislike roiling in his voice.

I rubbed my face, sighing. "Papa, I know. But you've gotta listen," I stated, waiting with arms crossed for him to settle down and hear me out.

Finally he did, arms crossed to mirror me, fidgeting. His eyes were frustrated. "Fine." He said. "Speak y'piece."

I dipped my head thankfully. "Well, Papa, they *are* my grandparents, and I've never even met them as such." Papa glowered at me, shaking his head, but I plowed through. "Besides, I went and *stole* one of their photographs! You can't expect me to pretend that didn't happen." I said expectantly.

What I didn't tell him was that I wanted to ask them their side of everything. Not that I didn't believe my Papa; I'd pick him over that awful woman any day! However, I wanted to ask the elderly couple quite a few questions. Like, *How could you miss your own daughter's funeral?*

Papa threw his hands up in the air and sighed, then rubbed his eyes with his palms. "Alright," He said, swallowing a few times, "alright."

I exhaled, not having realized that I'd been holding my breath. I felt a bit dizzy. "One more thing, Papa," I said firmly, even though I didn't quite manage to hide my wince. He raised his eyebrows.

"We gotta tell Lily at some point. Maybe not yet, but some day."

CHAPTER TWENTY-THREE

Papa and I, with heavy hearts, left the fields for now, headed for the house. Weeding could be done later tonight or tomorrow. Both of us knew what really had to be done.

As we walked, I tried to relax. My emotions were overflowing inside me – anger for the secrets, fear of change and confrontation, desperation to know the truth, loss for an Uncle I never knew, and longing for a mother who was gone.

All of this was dredging up the past, forcing us to *talk* about Mama. Talking about her and thinking about her were two very different things. Just echoing her existence, in my mind, would allow me to keep the tears inside me. I wasn't so sad about her death anymore – I felt a peace about it that went beyond all things earthly – but I still *missed* her, and I would for the rest of my life.

Speaking of her wasn't something we did all that often. If it were, we'd all be heartbroken, all the time. We'd had to allow time to heal the scars, and not re-open the wounds. That had meant forgetting, at least in a daily sense; forgetting where she would have been throughout our day, forgetting the things she'd have said, forgetting *her* on a daily basis. We'd forgotten her in this sense, just so that the echoes of Mama didn't haunt our waking moments the way they did our dreams.

It was a way to cope with the huge void left by loss, one we had no choice in. We could either forget, or lose ourselves remembering.

Sharp trickles of pain still crawled across my heart whenever I heard Mama's name, Rosalyn. It was sweet like honey, yet it sent daggers through my lungs, catching and stealing my breath.

Papa had called her Rose, and he'd insisted on naming at least one of their daughters after another flower. I smiled. Mama called him silly, but Papa said they could have a little flower just like her. So years after Mama picked my name, Papa chose Lily's name. Mama almost always called her Little Flower.

My heart felt like it was carrying something heavy with trembling arms. We were arriving home. Papa opened the door heavily and we walked inside. Willie was sitting on the couch. He looked up.

"Oh, howdy," he said. 'I were just takin' a break." His clothes were dusty and his shoes were scuffed, and I noticed the way he was sitting, like he was hurtin' real bad. I smiled at him.

"Hey, Willie. We were just about t'go on an errand, and we wanted to check in with somebody first." I looked meaningfully at Papa. He shrugged.

"So," I continued to Willie, "we'll be back when we're back. Keep an eye out, and tell Lily that we shouldn't be long if she asks."

Willie waved good-bye at us as we turned around and headed back out the door. Originally I had assumed we'd come in and get cleaned up before we visited the Johanssons. Then I realized, why should we care what they think? We were honest, hard-working folk, and they'd have to respect that. I squared my shoulders and walked taller. Then I slumped over as I realized we *weren't* so honest, apparently. Papa hadn't told me of my own grandparents. I glanced at him, and my stomach turned.

But we'd been over this. Papa was just afraid of ruining Mama's memory, and I understood him, leastaways, sort of. I didn't get how he could think that one secret would change my view of Mama forever. *I'd never let that happen,* I thought, shaking my head. But I did understand that he was just trying to protect his absent wife.

Forlornly, I stared out across the plains, seeing the Johanssons' low cabin stretched out on the dusty horizon. I sniffed the air, and it smelled wet and hot, somehow. Maybe another rain storm was on the way! Hope flared inside me. The crops needed as much water as possible.

As we walked, I glanced over at Papa repeatedly. I jumped as he said, "Why y'lookin' at me like that?"

I clucked aloud, saying, "I ain't really sure, Papa. Just thinking."

He squinted at me and then finally sighed and we kept walking.

Finally, after many minutes of frosty silence, we reached the Johanssons'. I dreaded the log cabin. It made my heart hurt in every way, remembering what they'd done to Mama, how they'd treated me. Papa strode up to the door and knocked on it. One of the curtains in the window swept aside, and half of a wrinkled face peered out at us. Then a very irritated Mrs. Johansson opened the door.

"Just what is it that you people want?" she snarled nastily. Then she looked at me and wrinkled her nose in disgust. "Have you brought the thief back?"

Papa stiffened and spoke sharply, trying to hide his anger. "Ma'am, we got some words t' exchange wit' you," he said. With a glance at me, he added, "Alex knows 'bout... all o' it."

Mrs. Johansson recoiled in distaste, screwing up her eyes and adjusting her hair bun with one strict hand. "You told her about us, did you?" She sniffed appraisingly. "I suppose it's never too late for a grandmotherly touch." And she smiled at me in a sticky, unused kind of way. I wilted away from her.

She smelled like sour bread.

Papa brushed his hand off on his pants and then offered it to the woman. She ignored it until he pulled it back, and he swallowed and asked, "C'we come in?"

She pulled her lips back in a smile and stepped back from the door. "Certainly." Papa and I glanced at each other and then stepped into the old cabin.

"Mr. Johansson is out chopping firewood," Mrs. Johansson said in a honey-sweet voice. "My company will have to do."

Her eyes reminded me of black pits. They were dark and small and seemingly endless, like you could fall into them if you weren't careful, and nobody'd ever be able to save you. Mrs. Johansson was staring at me pointedly. I started.

"Uh, I'm sorry, what?" I babbled. Mrs. Johansson shook her head with annoyance and frowned.

"Young lady, I *asked* you if you returned our photograph," she said in a superior way.

I balked. "I, ah, yes," I said, slowly drawing the photo out of my clothes. "But I'm afraid it's slightly damaged–"

The woman snatched it out of my hand. "Oh, oh dear, now, what a shame," she sighed like an empty tree rustling in the wind. "One of the few images of your mother that we had, all ruined, ink run and smudged and watered down. And it isn't as if we could just have another taken," she added in a crucial voice.

I shrank away from her in guilt, and Papa began sternly, "Ma'am, that's more'n enough."

Mrs. Johansson licked her lips and cleared her mouth. Speaking slowly, she stared pointedly at my papa. "Enough of what, sir?" She said, somehow insulting Papa without even saying s'much as an unkind word.

Papa changed his tune, attempting to turn her attention to the matter at hand. "Ma'am, please. The photograph ain't damaged that badly. We just came t'have a few civil words with you 'bout a few things of import," he said.

Mrs. Johansson tilted her head up and her little eyes waited. "Then speak. I do have other things to fill my time."

I could hardly believe that this was the woman my mama grew up with. *My* mama! The woman full of love and gentleness and soft, quiet strength. How'd she turn out the way she did, growing up in a snake's den? I cleared my mouth and prepared to speak.

"My mama left you," I began. "And I came here today to understand why. Why would she hide my uncle from me? Why would she pretend you all were just neighbors? I don't get it," I said, shaking my head. I really didn't. I wasn't trying to make my grandmother feel bad or condemn her; I just wanted to know the *whole* truth.

Mrs. Johansson scoffed prissily at me. "Why, how improper! You come here and insult me, and demand answers to questions you've no business asking," she huffed quickly. I took this as a sign that there was something more here, so I pushed harder.

"Why would a woman like my mama," I pressed carefully, "have to forget anyone?"

Mrs. Johansson looked coldly down at me, all the panic gone from her dark, pitiless eyes. "Your mother learned no respect. No respect at all for a woman's life or a woman's place, no idea how to act like a lady in public, or private for that matter! And she had *no* clue," she spat, "how to choose a husband."

Her eyes bored into us both. I dared to glance at Papa, eyes wide. He just raised his chin and sighed, rubbing it. It had to be the last straw – this woman disrespected his long-gone wife and declared him unfit as a husband. But my papa hadn't gotten angry. He'd just sighed, shaking his head. I sat and wondered about that. I wanted to ask him later, why hadn't he gotten angry? Could that always be done? Could anger always be corralled and channeled into something less harmful?

But Mrs. Johansson directed my attention for now. She was narrowing her eyes thoughtfully at me. "You look like her," she observed. I jumped, the words creeping through me like ice cold slivers.

"W-what?" I said, half-startled.

She nodded and sat back in her chair, satisfied. Papa narrowed his eyes. "You look just like her," she repeated. "Same wide nose, thin lips, pointy face." My cheeks burned. What was this woman saying?

"Mama was very pretty," I said softly. I wasn't entirely sure why we were lingering here. Papa glanced at me, and I lifted my head a little, wondering if we should leave.

Instead I steeled myself. There was something I wanted to say. I sat and waited and thought, and listened to the woman try to make proper conversation about market prices and the weather and how I should pick up sewing. Mrs. Johansson had just lapsed right back into her practiced little façade after her rude outburst. Papa and I exchanged regular glances, and I kept shaking my head, asking him to wait as the anger built inside me. I was trying to channel it into something less harmful.

Finally I held up a finger, and she halted for a moment, peering at me.

"Have you something of importance to say?" She said in a fluttery way. I nodded.

"What did you do to Mama, that she left you?" I asked, my voice decisively clear. "What did you do that she banned you from *me*?"

Mrs. Johansson sniffed primly. "It was Rosalyn who left, you know," she pointed out snidely. "It was her who left you."

For a moment I sat there and stared, unable to understand what she meant. Then her words clicked into place.

"You're blaming her for *dying?*" I cried, spitting with anger. Papa looked stunned, mouth half-open, unable to speak.

Mrs. Johansson just sat across from me, completely unfazed, and blinked a couple times. "The woman *was* being clumsy with a lantern, I've heard," she said matter-of-factly.

That was when I couldn't hold it together anymore. My feelings erupted, sadness pouring from my eyes and staining my vision. Mrs. Johansson crooked her neck in surprise.

"Young lady…" She began. I held up a hand and she drew back, indignant.

I mustered quiet dignity. Tears were still streaming down my face – a messy, hot mash-up of all the emotions I'd felt recently. Anger, pain, sorrow, loss, longing. All of them, a whirlwind of dislike and worry and anxiety. They poured out of me in liquid tears, my body wanting to shake with sobs. I was overcome.

Papa's eyes gleamed with fury at Mrs. Johansson for so abusing his daughter, "Now, you jus' wait a minute–"

But I stopped him. "It's okay, Papa." I said, looking him in the eyes, sniffing. Then I got up. I stood before that woman and I spoke with as much self-respect as I could scrape together.

My face flushed hot. "Mrs. Johansson, Mama was a score'n a half more the woman, the proper lady, the mother and the human being you are. She was your *daughter*, and you didn't even go to her funeral."

My voice was really low and cracked as I spoke. I felt oddly warm. "You may have wasted the only time you could've had with Mama," I said, chills arcing up my spine, "but I didn't. I remember her, and I'll keep remembering her as she was." My words strengthened and became clearer.

"I won't let you or nobody else tell the world who my mama was unless they're telling the truth. Mama was good, and she *loved me*." My mouth twitched in a frown, my muscles wanting to cry.

"She loved me! That's more than she could say from you. That's all that matters, all that ever mattered." Papa was watching in proud, stunned silence.

Mrs. Johansson's eyes had gotten bigger and bigger as I spoke, her eyebrows arched in indignation. She looked ready to burst, but as she opened her mouth, I held up a hand for her to be silent.

"Just let us leave, ma'am. I don't wanna be here anymore. I'll save you having to answer. We're just gonna leave now. I had to set y'right about Mama, a proclamation o'sorts, not the beginnings of an argument. Now my questions have answers."

And then I said the words that hurt but helped. "I wish somebody'd show you the love Mama showed me. I hope they do. You were right; it's never too late, Mrs. Johansson. We're still your neighbors. Maybe there's more we can be."

Her face had turned red, but I didn't care. I turned and trotted out the door, feeling lighter than I had in a long time. The emotions, the fear and pain and worry, a lot of them were gone. They'd been washed away by my tears. I was sorry the visit hadn't gone better, sorry I'd been backed into defending Mama like that. I felt forced and empty but lighter.

Mama's memory was too precious to let her own mother spit at it. I couldn't take that... I set my jaw to keep my mouth from trembling. Papa had walked out behind me, grinning like a kid let out of school early.

He was still shaking his head, and he cleared his throat roughly. "Alex, that were somethin' else." He half-laughed, half-coughed.

I looked at my hand, watched its tremors. My eyes were wide. "I wasn't telling her off or anything, honest. Didn't even yell," I said quietly. Papa nodded. "But that woman needed to know a few things, like how lucky she was to have such a daughter." My words were soft.

"And how foolish she been t' throw that away," Papa finished, looking at the ground. I nodded at him and felt more tears brimming in my eyes. Papa looked back to me and I hugged him quickly. He patted my head fondly. Letting go, I stared back the way we'd come.

"Let's go home," I said wearily.

CHAPTER TWENTY-FOUR

I didn't even want to think about my grandmother anymore, or my absent grandfather with nothing to say. So when we got home that night, I went straight to bed and slept. I fell asleep quickly, unburdened, at least for a night. I was glad of the way I'd defended Mama. Her memory was always going to be something important to me; I couldn't let someone just tarnish it like that. Mama was... she was my mama. I loved her. We all did.

That night, I dreamed.

Lily was sick again, and so was Willie. They wailed out at me in dead voices, crying for food and water. They clawed at me with thin, cut-up hands. I scrambled away from them, terrified, and felt ashamed that I didn't care. That I wanted them to die so I wouldn't have to worry anymore.

Then Lily and Willie melted away, and I was standing on the plains, a field before me. I was lugging water to crops. Back and forth from a river, for hours. As I turned away for the last time, leaving the fields, I felt heat behind me. I turned, mouth open, ready to scream, as the crops burned up into ash before me and vanished like lightning from the sky.

I woke up screaming.

Papa rushed in, flicking on the light. *It must be morning,* I thought dimly, *else the electricity would probably be out.*

It was early – darkness streamed in from the window, sliding off against the light, slinking back from whence it came.

Papa's startled face peered down at me. "Alex! Whatcha screamin' for?"

I hesitated and shook my head. "Just a bad dream, Papa," I said, shuddering. It was already fading from my mind – all I could see were chaotic flashes of Willie fading away, burning crops, and Lily's pale, sickly face.

"Are you sure?" Papa asked cautiously. I glanced up at him.

"Positive," I sighed. "I can't even remember it anymore." He watched me for a moment more and then nodded, turning away. I saw him go and then tunneled under the covers of my bed.

I was tired, but sleep evaded me now. It was early and my exhaustion was deep in my bones, but with the memory of the dream's darkness, I found more rest hard to come by. Sighing for the millionth time, I slumped out of bed and stepped heavily down the hallway, headed to the kitchen.

I began breakfast automatically, my hands taking things and boiling water and dumping oats into a pot. I started to think about Willie, remembering the day he'd confided in me his lack of faith. I mentally paused. He didn't truly *not* believe, did he? The whole morning sped by me, and then we were sitting at the table, finishing our meal and talking. Well, Willie, Lily and Papa were talking. I was thinking.

To me, it seemed as though Willie was just hurting. Remembering his pa and wishing for his ma. He was just confused and angry. It had to hurt, being an orphan. I shivered involuntarily.

"Alex?" said someone.

"Huh?" I managed.

"I said, you cold or somethin'?" Asked a confused Willie.

"N-no," I stuttered, completely caught off guard. "No, I just, was thinking about all the dish-washing Lily's gonna have to do to keep up with you lot!"

This prompted a few laughs and I relaxed a bit. Papa stood and began clearing his dishes, ever the first to begin his day.

"Well," he said, clomping to the kitchen, "I'm off to town today. You lot get your chores done at some point, y'hear?" He reminded us.

We all chorused, "Yes, Papa," and laughed. I smiled at the way Willie was one of us now. Upon hearing the front door slam, Willie said mischievously, "I says we get into the cupboards 'n make off w' Papa's food!"

Lily snorted. "Bubba, his food is *our* food."

Willie pulled a face. "Darn, you're right."

I looked at him humorously and then began piling dishes. "We do have to get on with our day, though," I said matter-of-factly.

Willie stuck his tongue out at me and crossed his eyes. Then he let his face relax and sniffed properly. "I don't see why you lot git to use me as a human slave," he complained. "I do gots my own things to accomplish, people to see." He gestured grandly.

I snickered. "What, you gonna go lay in the shadows until you're all pale again?"

Willie stuck his nose up at me. "Maybe I am, Alexandria," he snorted.

I rolled my eyes. "Lily, go gather the laundry from the rooms. Willie and I will take care of clearing the table."

"'Ey, speak for y'self," Willie protested, even as he started to pick up dishes. We dubiously cleared the table as Lily flounced away to gather clothing to wash.

I glanced uncomfortably at my friend. "Willie, I've been meaning to talk to you, you know," I said uncertainly. A shadow crossed his face, but it was gone in moments.

"What d'you want now, Alex?" He joked half-heartedly. I felt sad.

"I wanna help you understand... God, and everything," I said softly. "'Cause I want you to be royalty with me again."

Willie's mouth tightened and he looked away from me, eyes dark. "What makes you think I wanna understand," he muttered.

I tried to fight the despair in his eyes as it clawed at me. "Don't say that, Willie. You're just mad at God. And that's okay!" I cried. "He can take it!"

Willie glanced up at me uncertainly. "But... ain't 'e mad at me?"

I shook my head in disbelief. "What for, Willie?"

He ground his teeth and looked at his feet. "For lettin' Pa die." His voice was heavy and low. I felt cold grip my heart.

"No, Willie," I whispered. "That's not your fault."

He turned viciously to me and hissed, "Didn't ye blame yoreself? When y'ma died?"

I stuttered, "Well, I, but..."

"No buts!" Willie cried. "Yes or no?" His voice was hysterical, almost desperate, like he needed to know his emotions were human.

I looked at him. "Yeah, Willie, I did. For a long, long time."

He relaxed. "There, see? I ain't unnatural. It were my fault, to me, anyway, and ain't nothin' gonna change that," he said stubbornly.

"But Willie," I protested. "That isn't a burden you gotta carry around with you. You're not alone. Let me tell you something. I haven't told anybody yet, aside from Papa, because nobody's asked, but I was awake when Lily was healed. I saw it all."

His eyes got bigger and bigger as I recounted the story as best I could remember. When I finished, he whispered, "You saw one? An angel?"

I nodded. My words were weak.

Willie collapsed into a chair in disbelief and wonder. "It was really like that, then? All light and, what'd ye say, purity?" I nodded again.

"Did it have wings?" asked Willie in awe.

Something inside me realized that he had just believed me instantly, which got me thinking. If Willie *really* didn't believe, he wouldn't have just accepted my miraculous story. It convinced me – Willie just needed time to make things right with God. His lack of faith wasn't the issue, it was him trying to reason out a God bigger than anything we could imagine. Not to mention the pain he felt inside over his pa. I was afraid that he hated himself for it.

"Wings..." I said, squinting, trying to remember every detail clearly. "Yeah... Huge. Huge wings. Multiple pairs. They touched the edges of the room." I said, blinking as I tried to recall it. "But there was so much light, it was more like just a figure. Standing, or floating, I guess, kinda just *being* there, in front of me." I knew my words were sloppy and indistinct, but it was the best I could do to recapture the incredible scene I had been witness to.

"And let me tell you something, Willie," I added, shivering. "That angel was unlike *anything* that we've *ever* been told angels were." He blinked at me. "It was huge, and powerful, so beyond me..." I breathed shallow. "But it told me not to be afraid."

Willie closed his eyes, smiling. "I wanna see an angel someday," he said. "I wanna see one just like that, all light an' goodness an' strength."

I looked on in happiness. "You can, Willie. You gotta want Jesus as your savior," I insisted. "He'll take you places and show you things you haven't ever seen." Willie opened his eyes, listening. I took his silence as a sign to continue.

"God wants the best for you, Willie, honest," I said with sincerity. "He wants to give you everything that *you* want. But you gotta let him lead you, and even when things turn tough..." Willie's eyes were downcast. "...you gotta do your best to just *trust* Him. 'Cause sometimes you won't be able to understand what's goin' on or why bad things happen, and trusting Him is what we gotta turn to. It's called faith, and everything will turn out the better for it. Not just here, in our temporary lives, but in Heaven. Life is eternal there," I smiled. "We never have to leave or lose our loved ones, and life just goes on and on without hardship or awful things like sickness and death, or jealousy, or pain, or hatred. We all live and love and *enjoy* every moment of it, forever. Kings and Queens and Princes and Princesses of the Most High."

Willie was looking at me in wonder, head tilted to the side. "Is it really like that, Alex?" He asked softly.

I nodded, smiling broadly. "It is. Everything we've seen of God," I said, gesturing around me, "everything we've been through and survived, all of it tells of His nature. He's a lover, and a King, and a fighter, all in one," I said. "He himself is fire and love. His love burns like flames for us. And with that love He built us a beautiful world, with beautiful free will to be who we are inside. Why wouldn't He make a wonderful place for us to dwell with Him forever, past the end of time? His son died for us, died to release us from the grip of our sins. Don't you see how amazing that is?" I said, beaming. "He's done so much for us, and all we have to do is take the hand He's extended to us, follow him, and be His. Heaven is real," I said firmly, "as real as Hell and evil are. As solid as darkness and death can be, so much brighter is the light that came to set us free." I laughed because the words rhymed.

Willie was staring down at the floor. "How do I ask 'im to lemme be... royalty?" he asked me, sad longing in his voice.

Absolute joy rushed through me. I took his hands. "Like this," I said, placing his hands together in prayer position. "Close your eyes."

Willie obeyed and I said, "Just say what I say. We're just talkin' to God. Even if you don't feel it, He's with us. He's callin' you to him, and He'll take it from here."

He took a deep breath. "Okay."

I began slowly, "Father, I'm not perfect."

"Father, I'm... I ain't perfect."

"I've done wrong things. I believe in your son, Jesus, who died to wash those sins clean from me." Willie echoed me. "But I want to ask You to please get rid of my sins, now and forever and in the future, 'cause I wanna be a part of Your family now. I accept Jesus as my savior and my path to You." Willie sighed softly and repeated what I said.

"Please come into my life and make me whole, Lord, and help me follow You all my days." Slowly and clearly, Willie spoke my words. He had dropped to the floor, kneeling. I was finished and just about to say, *Amen,* when he kept going.

"God, I ain't real close t'you," he stated, "but I sure wanna be, I think. Wait, no," he said, shaking his head. "I do. I do wanna know you." I couldn't help smiling.

"Be part o' my life now, Lord," he said shakily. "show me how t' be good to folk like Papa an' Lily an' Alex." My heart ached.

"I... dunno how t'do this..." Willie faltered. "Jus' help me be a better son, t'you and Papa, God. Even when somethin' real awful happens, help me trust You, even t' the end." He dropped his head and his voice was small. "I need You. Amen."

I knelt to hug him. "That was right beautiful, Willie," I said, my eyes misty. "You're safe forever, now." We both beamed at that, and half-laughed, half-cried.

Safe forever.

I didn't have to worry anymore.

CHAPTER TWENTY-FIVE

Life flew by after that. Every moment was full of joy and happiness; my family was whole and complete. I had made my peace with Mama and her secrets, and everything was beautiful. Lily was healed, and Willie was saved. Time just sort of slipped by us. Days, weeks, months passed. Every Sunday, all four of us went to church. Willie had absolutely no problem with anything godly, not anymore. He loved the relationship he was cultivating with our Father.

We all went to another Founder's Day Festival, enjoying the friendship and food and games. Those boys didn't bother Willie anymore. Lily simply *reveled* in every waking moment; I doubted that she would ever again take anything for granted, even things as daily as walking or eating. Her perspective was simply changed, for the better, it seemed. We enjoyed everything about our lives. And it wasn't until these months of joy and peace had gone by that times began to truly grow worse...

It wasn't until later that the dust truly came.

"Willie!" I yelled. "You in here?" The door slammed shut behind me as I strode into the kitchen, clomping the dirt out of my shoes.

A curly red head popped up around the corner from the front room, eyes dim with drowsiness. "I reckon," he said sleepily. "I was just takin' a nap. M'chores are all finished, 'course."

I chuckled. "Well, wake up, curly. We've got a supper to prepare."

Willie yawned, stretching, and padded shakily into the kitchen. He sniffed. "Smells like wet dog in here," he complained. I rolled my eyes.

"You sure that ain't you, Willard?" I snorted.

He fake laughed. "Aha ha ha, Alex. " Then he stuck his tongue out at me and made a ridiculous face, and I giggled.

"Careful, your face will stick like that. You'll end up looking like a miggun for the rest of your days."

He looked confused. "What's a miggun?"

I felt startled, frowning. What *was* a miggun? It had just been in my head... My expression cleared as the memory presented itself, and I smiled, remembering Willie sneaking up on me in the summer that so-long-ago day.

"Nothing at all," I murmured, lost in memories. Our time with Willie had flown by. He had so fully become a member of the family that none of us even realized he'd been with us over a year by now. It was truly amazing. I felt so grateful that Willie was part of our family now; he was our brother.

Lily was overly fond of him, calling him 'Bubba', immensely glad to have a brother. Willie loved it. I smiled, thinking how he'd gained two sisters and a father, after he'd lost the last of his only family. My eyes watered and I coughed. Willie looked up at me from the water he was boiling on the stove.

"You alright? Steam blowin' in your eyes?"

I scoffed. "There ain't no steam even rising yet, Willie. You dumb creature." Willie cackled.

"I see plenty o' hot air... Comin' outta your ears!"

I made a 'you're-so-funny' face at him and went to the pantry to look for something to boil. I was faced with a near-empty pantry. A jar of peanuts next to a line of canned fruits stared down at me, along with two bags of flour and a loaf of bread I'd baked yesterday. Was this all we had?

My mouth set in a deep frown, I turned back to face Willie. "There's less and less food every day."

He stared past me at the lacking pantry. "Looks like plenty there t'me."

I rolled my eyes at him. "Willie, a few bags o' flour and some bread ain't gonna last too long around here." Phantom pangs of hunger gripped my stomach, predicting the inevitable. Our crops were starving. Were we next? I'd been slowly worrying about this for weeks, feeling the food in the pantry slip away, trying to forget and hope for the best. But it had all been piling up inside me and now I felt ready to snap.

"What are we gonna do?" I asked, sliding down against a wall. "What is there to do?"

"Calm down," Willie said, shaking his head. "There ain't no need to panic."

I stopped, staring at him, disbelief seeping out through my clenched teeth. "No need to panic? Calm down?" I repeated. "Yes," he said, shrugging. "Gotta have faith, Alex." His words bounced around in my head but didn't stay. The fear was too strong.

"I don't know what to do. I'll have to talk to Papa. Maybe I can start workin' in town for somebody who can afford to pay me, I can make some money and we'll have to start buyin' food," I rambled, planning and analyzing like I'd always done.

Willie raised his hands in protest. "Alex, woah. Nobody's goin' to work in town, leastaways not 'til we talk to Papa. Have some faith," he insisted.

"I know what's going to happen." My earlier thoughts echoed and I spoke them selfishly. "Our crops are starvin', and we're next."

I rubbed my eyes in defeat as Willie stared. "Alex," he said slowly. I waited, slightly annoyed at his silence. "Y'can't say things like that when they ain't true," he said carefully.

"Why not?" I asked sharply, a flash of fear-fed anger awakening in me. After everything we'd been through, hunger was gonna defeat us?

"Can't eat dust, Willard. Though that might be faster'n starvin'." Willie drew in a sharp breath, his eyes staring past me.

"Now you done it," he muttered.

I turned.

Lily stood there, soft brown eyes stark with shock. She stared at me for a moment, shaking her head, and then she turned and ran.

"Oh no," I said softly.

CHAPTER TWENTY-SIX

Lily's face was buried in her pillow. I opened my mouth to speak but then shut it, shaking my head worriedly. I glanced back at Willie who had followed me into the room.

"Lily?" I asked softly. "You okay?"

Lily just threw her arms over her head, curled up in a ball on the bed.

"Lil Monster," Willie said gently. "you gotta look at us."

Lily held her pillow tighter for a moment and then slowly sat up and looked at us. Her eyelashes were dark with tears.

"You said we were gonna starve. And it's Papa's fault?" She sniffed, quivering.

"No, no!" I cried. "Oh, Lily, it's not like that at all. I just got scared, Lil," I said desperately. Lily's eyebrows were down, her sad eyes accusing me.

"But you.. you said we've got no food left," Lily stumbled over her words, still half-crying.

"Lily, please, I'm sure... we'll be okay," I insisted, searching perilously for words to comfort her.

Lily gazed up at me, scrubbing at her eyes. "Promise?" She sniffed. I smiled in relief, glad to have reassured her fragile anxieties, at least for the moment. She was still just a kid.

"I promise," I breathed, hugging Lily to me. Willie looked on quietly.

After a moment longer, I released my younger sister. "Alright," I said softly. "You just take your time, Lily." I patted her on the back. "Everything will be just fine." Willie and I turned to leave.

As soon as we were in the hall, Willie turned to me seriously, eyes dark with worry. "Are y'gonna be okay?" He asked.

I took a deep breath. "Yeah. Everything just kinda got to me. Thanks for not crumblin' too."

He relaxed, nodding. I couldn't miss the joy on his face. "Faith, Alex," he said, almost laughing with the sureness of it all. "We ain't never gotta be afraid." I clenched my teeth together and nodded. But doubt had begun to creep into my heart, and fear was its constant companion.

The day was long in my head. Every moment that passed I spent worrying about our dwindling resources. We used to always enjoy a full cupboard, just 'cause our eggs and milk had been plenty for us trade with. But after weeks of denial, I'd truly seen how it was now; nearly bare. Worry stalked my every action, filling me with dread whenever something reminded me of our situation. Long, long minutes crawled by as I waited for Papa to return. I knew I needed to talk to him.

Willie and I were standing in the fields staring at the crops at the moment, lamenting all the work we'd been doing to no avail.

"I don't know why we even bother," I grumbled. "They're all dying!" I threw my hands up in frustration, eyes wide with regret. Willie wiped his nose on the back of his hand and looked around.

"Well, yeah," He admitted. "They kinda are." Long rows of wilting potato plants affronted us. After last season's pitiful harvest and the way the corn had been destroyed, we'd decided on a hardier crop this year. But even the potatoes were giving in to the heat and the dust.

"They're just not getting enough water," I stated, scratching my ear. "How long is this drought going to go *on?*" I moaned, falling over onto the ground, staring hopelessly at the sky.

"Alex, yer crushin' some plants," Willie pointed out. I barely heard him.

After all this time, I had realized something. I'd been allowing myself blind happiness, when all the while our world was crumbling down around us. I knew the crops were failing, but I just kind of assumed that things would be alright, in the end. But now... with the food mostly gone, how would we survive the coming winter? The harvest was due in half a month, and then the days would begin to grow cold. My faith was ebbing like the tide.

"Alex, what're ya doin'?" Willie exclaimed. I let my head flop to the side to look at him.

"What?" I asked.

Willie made an exasperated noise. "You was makin' weird grumbling sounds," Wilie said. "I was scared." I rolled my eyes at him, not in the mood to laugh.

"I was just thinking, we're really losing everything here," I said, a sudden wave of despair washing over me. "No food, no crops, nobody to help us," I said, feeling empty. "What will we do?" I gazed at the sky, hearing no response. Then my skin began to prickle and I realized that Willie was glaring at me. Sitting up, I faced him.

"What!" I exclaimed. "Why're you looking at me like that?"

Willie's eyes were angry. "Alex, it's 'bout time you quit all this," he said slowly. "Ain't no time for givin' up."

I felt accosted. "Can't I complain once in a while?" I asked mutinously.

Willie shook his head. "This ain't complainin' of late. You been *givin' up*. And Alex don't give up none, ever." I stared at him.

"Alex, you a'member, some time past, when you told me I gotta keep trustin' God, when things don't make no sense and when everything looks right like the whole world's comin' down on y'shoulders?" I nodded numbly.

"Well," he continued, "it's your turn. And I know y'got it in ya," he added. "You done it afore."

Thoroughly chastened, I stood and pulled Willie up to a standing position with me. "You're right, Bubba. Let's go inside." Simple as that, we turned and walked inside, all fear forgotten, at least for the moment.

It was nearly dark out when Papa finally made it home. Long shadows were twisting and moving slowly outside, gaining purchase on the day that was quietly setting. Red-tinged light stole over the horizon as the sun went down, setting the sky aflame. While I felt a ghostly remnant of a shiver, my memories were overshadowed by the brilliant majesty of the burning sky. I was no longer saddened by the sunset.

When at last Papa strode through the doorway, Lily was asleep and Willie and I waited in the front room for him. He was too late for supper, but there hadn't been any anyway. I didn't dare waste the few supplies we had left.

"Papa." I said as he walked in. "We've been waiting for you."

He raised his eyebrows. "What for, Alex? Y'should be in bed now, y'know."

I swallowed hard. "Papa, I've been ignorin' it for a while now, but I don't see how we can go much longer with what little food we've got left." Papa inclined his head slightly at me and opened his mouth to answer, but suddenly the words were tumbling out of me and I couldn't control my mouth.

"I don't know what to do, Papa. I should've said somethin' earlier. We can't just *starve*," I cried. "There's gotta be somethin' we can do! I'm so scared," I admitted, and my breath was heaving with despair. Papa looked beleaguered, and kind of like he knew somethin' I didn't.

Papa shook his head. "Alex, Willie, c'mon now with me." With that he turned and walked out the door, and Willie and I, perplexed as ever, trotted right out after him, too curious to question our destination. We set out in the darkness, and a million queries throbbed in my mind like an infected cut. Where were we going?

But that question was answered before too long. The barn loomed huge and dark before us in the twilight, looking slightly forbidding with its sloping roof and shadowy exterior. Papa slipped up to it and pulled the door open, motioning us inside. What could possibly be here to help us? I hesitated, but

Willie just vanished into the shadows without a moment's thought. I stepped cautiously into the darkness, my eyes feeling big and bright in the shadows.

Sudden, flickering light leapt onto the walls and around us as Papa lit a lantern in his hand that he'd pulled off a wall hook. Something massive was crouched in front of us, bulky and awkwardly shaped and strange-looking in the dancing colors of the lantern.

"Whazzat?" asked Willie, peering closely at it. I tensed, waiting for the monster to snatch Willie up in one huge claw.

"That," smiled Papa, "that's our ticket outta here." And with that he whipped off a tarp, revealing stacks and stacks of cans and boxes and jars and great big sacks in rows and everything all crammed on one large cart of some sort...

"Papa," I breathed. "what is all this?"

Papa looked triumphantly over the supplies, joy battling weariness on his tough, lined face. "Everythin' we need t'start over," he said softly. The lantern played mysterious beams of light over his tired eyes, and they gleamed in the dark.

"What do you mean, start over?" Echoed Willie.

"I mean," clarified Papa, "that we're leavin' this place. Headin' west, afore the dust goes thicker. Soon's I can find us a ride west."

I looked up at Papa, terrified, electrified. "Leave? Everything?"

He nodded. "It'll be tougher'n any journey y'can imagine, but here ain't no home to us no more. Too much darkness. We gonna find somewhere better." I gaped at the supplies. We weren't going to starve at all.

We were leaving?

CHAPTER TWENTY-SEVEN

Lily was surprisingly okay with leaving. She was pretty excited, in fact. Thinking about it, I realized that this place probably didn't hold much in the way of fond memories for her. She had been too young to remember much about Mama, but what she could recall probably wasn't very pleasant. I shook myself and sighed, trying to feel happier. We were leaving this place! I still couldn't quite take it all in. The pain, the memories, the dust. We were leaving all of it behind as soon as possible for a brighter beginning.

I took a deep breath, forcing myself to smile. The day was bright outside, the world flooded with golden sunlight that made everything seem sharp and new. My ears pricked as I heard a rumbling from outside – sounded like an engine. My blood picking up, I rushed outdoors and stood by the front step. Papa was out front already, dusting off his jeans and looking expectantly at the road.

"What is it, Papa?" I spoke quietly. He shook his head.

"Don't rightly know," he answered, eyes narrowed. Why would anyone be coming to see us in a vehicle? We didn't know many people with cars. Just Farmer Thompson with his brown truck that he let us use in exchange for the use of our field equipment, but we always walked over to pick that up. At that moment, a rust-red pick-up truck rounded a corner in the road and rumbled up onto our drive. I stared at the driver's seat.

Mr. Johansson, my grandfather, sat there, rough old hands clutching the wheel, bushy eyebrows drawn together. He shifted the truck into park and clambered out slowly. Rubbing his eyes, he wandered up to us almost sheepishly and asked if he might come inside. Papa and I exchanged huge glances. Numbly, I heard him invite the large old man inside. I trailed them silently.

We all sat down at the kitchen table, and Grandfather crossed and uncrossed his burly arms and coughed roughly, sounding like he'd swallowed sandpaper. He stared at the wood knots in the table for a moment, his old eyes hidden beneath drooping silver brows. Papa and I glanced at one another, and the awkward moment stretched out. Papa cleared his throat, about to offer the man something to eat or drink. Blood rushed inside me when I remembered we could afford to share our food, because we really weren't going to starve. We were *leaving*. My heart jumped up a notch.

Grandfather finally looked up at us, and he raised his eyes and we could see their tired, dark surfaces. He stroked his gray beard with one hand and then dropped his arm.

"It was so hard to come see you all today," he began. His voice was low and unpolished, rough from disuse. I tensed, waiting for some accusation or for him to demand that we give him something.

"There'll never be a thing I can do to make up for my silence." He lowered his head again, and I felt everything in me freeze in shock at the sound of tears in his voice. Papa started to say something, but Mr. Johansson cut him off, straightening up.

"I've stood by all these years. For so long, I watched my wife verbally abuse our daughter, and her family, and..." he choked off. Papa and I waited in stunned silence. "I even let that godless old woman keep me from my own daughter's funeral," he said, and the void in his voice was so heavy that I felt my heart sinking.

"I've never been one to confront, you see," he rumbled, eyes low again, "and my wife has always taken care of any personal relations." He pulled his gaze up and met my Papa's eyes, and then turned to look into mine.

"I've been a coward." His hands trembled, and something in me suddenly felt as though he really was my grandpa. Tears slowly made their way down his face, and he shook his head, closing his eyes.

"I'll never, ever be able to see our Rosalyn again or apologize to her. I'll never be able to make that right." Grandfather's eyes opened, and suddenly his voice was steel, gaining a startling strength.

"But I am *finished* letting my wife destroy people," he said coldly. I wondered how it would feel to be in such a loveless relationship. It made me ache inside.

Papa began to nod. "It were you, then." He said, starting to smile. I stared at him in confusion, and then my gaze whipped to Grandfather as he started to speak.

"Yessir, that was me." The old man smiled hollowly. "It's one of the least things I can do." The two men sat there for a moment, Papa grinning and Grandfather gazing sadly at the wall. Both were lost in thought.

"Helloo?" I wondered aloud. "What on earth's goin' on?"

Papa turned to me. "Near ten days past, I rose w'the sun an' found that big ol' cart o'supplies waitin' by the front door. There were a paper sat atop w' scrawlins on it, said "For Rosalyn." Papa smiled again, shaking his head with a rough sigh.

"For long days, I'd been thinkin' we should get outta here. Wonderin'. Prayin'. But I didn't right have any idea how to go about stockpilin' all the goods we was gonna need."

He turned softly to Grandfather. "And then y'gift showed up, day after I decided t'start sellin' off what little we had t'pay for the way. But it would never 'ave been near enough."

Grandfather looked stunned. "You were already plannin' on goin'?" he asked, shocked.

Papa nodded. "It were a long time comin'. I needed a push, though. I were askin' God to show me what to do an' how." Grandfather sat back in his chair, shaking his head in wonderment.

Finally I spoke. "Grandpa?" I said haltingly. The word felt strange on my tongue.

He looked up, eyes watery. "If you'd like to call me that," he said softly, his mouth frownin' the way it does in tears.

I took a breath. "You're forgiven, Grandpa." I said quietly. "Mama would have forgiven you. And I do, too." Grandfather stared at me, eyes blazing with hopeful fire. Tears began to swell in his eyes.

"And also," I said fiercely, "don't say you'll never get to see her again!"

Silence.

"My Mama went to heaven, Grandpa! Your daughter is there *waiting for you*!" I cried. He took in a shuddering breath, tears all caught in his grayin' beard. His words were a whisper.

"I want to see her again." Sharp joy welled in me at the coming redemption of this man, my grandpa.

"Ask him, Grandpa. Ask the Lord to save you and take you home with him one day."

Papa was staring at me, nodding slowly, ferocious pride shining in his eyes for his daughter, and a touch of shame for my weeping grandpa. He was right embarrassed by all this open talk, but I knew Papa was well aware of how important this all was. Grandfather looked at me with ancient sorrow swimming in his gaze. But slowly, the light of faith began to touch his eyes. His bent his head so far, his gray-black beard brushed the table.

"God," he muttered. "I want to see my daughter again someday. I know I've been a pretty terrible follower, and I've not spoken to you in a long time. But..." he swallowed hard. "But I want to be yours again, God. Help me live the rest of my life as your child."

I glanced up at Grandfather, thinking he was done talking. But his eyes were still tightly shut, his head down. He sighed. "Lord..." He hesitated. "You've done some amazing things; I can see that, through this family here." I gave a tired smile.

"So God, I think you might be able to heal my wife..."

Papa and I waited in sharp silence. "She needs you more than anyone, God. Bitterness is so strong in her. Release her from it, God." He took a huge breath, exhaling it slowly, and then looked up at me.

I shook my head in wonder, eyes watering. "Perfect, Grandpa."

We all sniffed and rubbed at our eyes for a few moments. Papa coughed, refusin' to cry. What a talk.

Finally, Grandfather stroked his beard and cleared his throat, blinking hard. "Well now," he said. "well now. With all that emotion outta the way, I've got some pretty great news for you folk." He smiled at us then, and it was a real, genuine smile. I wondered how long it had been since that sagging old face had looked happy.

Papa looked at Grandfather in curiosity. "What is it, sir?"

"Where have you been storin' your food?" Grandfather answered Papa's question with a question.

Papa looked mystified. "The barn."

"Let's go!" Grandfather exclaimed, gesturing outside. So we stood and followed him back outside, where he got in the truck and told us to hop in the back. We obliged.

The old beast rumbled to life and Grandfather drove it toward the barn. Papa and I bounced along in the back in silence, watching the barn grow closer. Finally we stopped and jumped down. Grandfather told Papa to open the barn and roll out the cart of food. Looking as confused as ever, Papa did what he said. Grandfather nodded at the cart as it was pulled into the sunlight. I marveled once again at the hugeness of our supplies.

Then Grandfather gestured at the wide vehicle, smiling. "We gotta figure out how to hook up that cart to her. Gotta make sure it'll pull right. My ole truck is yours now."

I instantly looked to Papa, whose eyes were huge. He recovered first. "Sir, we can't letcha jus' give us this here truck for free." He stood straightbacked, unwilling to take a gift out of pity.

Grandfather shook his head. "I'm not giving it to you for free." I watched Papa as he considered the words. Grandfather lowered his head and became very small. "It was paid for many times over in hardship and pain." Papa seemed to give a very small nod, like he knew this was something my grandpa had to do. I saw the pride leave Papa's stance as he realized what this was to Grandfather. His shoulders were hunched, still hurting from his silence. Grandfather looked so sad and small that I hugged him.

"Thank you," I smiled up at his gray face. My smile was immediately returned.

Papa turned to Grandfather. "Let's figure how t'get this ole thing hitched," he grinned.

CHAPTER TWENTY-EIGHT

I was lying on my bed, staring at the ceiling. Gazing at the walls, the windows.

And that was when it hit me.

One week.

One week, and we'd be leaving everything I'd ever known. Pain lanced through me as I realized I would be losing more of my Mama than I could possibly recover from; how would I remember her in a new place that had never been touched by her loving grace? Even though many of my memories here were tainted in places by ash and darkness, I still clung to them with desperation. I didn't want to forget a moment with my mama, the one I would have to wait a lifetime to see again. I remembered how Willie had never known his mother, and felt impossibly weighted with sorrow. At least I'd *really* known my Mama. She had been my greatest ally, my teacher, my mother. I felt sick even trying to imagine never having met her.

Shaking my head, I blinked hard and wandered outside to sit on the steps. The very same steps that I had once stargazed on with Mama; one of the last places she had drawn breath. I sighed tiredly and dropped my head onto my knees, staring at the dusty ground. Wind swirled around me, and the soil flew up and danced about. I tensed, but it grew no worse at the moment. It was just the winds bearing away the dust, to form a devastating storm somewhere else.

I sat up and looked around. The sun was nearly gone beyond the horizon, and the darkness it left behind was tinged with golden tones, oddly enough. Normally, the Colorado air was burnt with fire as the sun set, but this evening, the great star left behind an aura of soft bronze. I gazed at it, head tilted sideways. I watched as the sun sank quietly, and the gold in the sky slowly vanished, leaving behind ever-so-faint tendrils of sparkling translucence on my eyelids.

I lay back on the steps. It was uncomfortable, but I didn't care. My heart felt like it was being squeezed. I had to say goodbye to this place. Without even thinking about it, words began to fall from my mouth, in sync with the stars slowly appearing in the chasm above me.

"Mama, I'm sorry." They were a breath of wind, the soft whisper of two clouds passing one another. I felt everything with the beat of my heart; the growing cries of the crickets, the faint pulsing light of the moon, the surreal swirling of the dust in the wind.

I felt the words of a poem rising in my mind, one Mama had taught me long ago. My breath caught as I realized its words and their connection to me.

Here upon the sunrise bold,
I cast my worries to the flames.
I cast my love and all I hold,
Into the dark, beyond this place.

Numbly, I felt the meaning sink in. The only difference was that it was sunset now, not sunrise. I knew what I was doing now. Why I had wandered out here. And in recognizing the desire of my heart, I took a breath and continued.

"Mama, I'm sorry we're leaving you behind." As I spoke the words, part of me knew they weren't true; part of me knew that she would be with me, forever, and that I'd be reunited with her someday. But no matter the truth of those words, I also felt like most of her would stay here in this town. I felt like her memory was trapped here, a haunting part of this town that would linger evermore. So I hardened my resolve to remember.

"God, please help me never, ever forget my Mama. Let her be with me no matter where I tread, Father. I want Mama with me," I breathed. Closing my eyes and clasping my hands together tight, I spoke my thoughts aloud. "Mama, I miss you so much. I don't know if you can hear me, but I think God will give you the message," I added.

"I want you to know that... that I'm trying really hard to be just the way you'd want me to be. I mean," I clarified, "that I'm trying to grow up like you. I wanna be smart, and kind, and wise. Oh, Mama, am I making you sound perfect? I know you weren't perfect," I hastened, afraid to make her feel bad. "I mean, I know you were pretty close," I added, smiling to myself. "But I want you to know that I forgive you for anything you maybe ever did wrong. I can't think of anything, but I just want you to know that if I could, I'd still forgive you. Oh, Mama, I miss you," I said, my voice thickening.

Talking like this was reminding me of the old days, when we'd sit on these steps and talk the days through. I remembered Mama telling me how she'd have enough love for both of us when she found out she was pregnant with Lily. My eyes misting up, I realized there had been plenty of love, but not nearly enough time. I wanted to wail it to the skies, "I want her back! I want her back *now*."

But I didn't. Instead, I took a breath and finished my talk with Mama. The last one I'd ever have on these steps. "Mama, I'm saying goodbye to this place, and all the bad memories here. From when... when you went away..." I trembled, trying to suppress the flashes of smoke and the screaming. "But I'm not saying goodbye to you, Mama." I took a deep breath and stood up.

"So, goodbye, house," I said, smiling and waving at our old home. I turned out to the fields and bid them goodbye without even a bit of remorse. No more fieldwork here! Finally I turned to the open land before me. "Goodbye, Colorado," I called. I wasn't going to miss the devastation caused by the dust storms. I wouldn't miss the bitter way I woke up every morning, the frustration of being unable to ever be truly clean. I hoped wherever we were going was cleaner than here. I took a final deep breath and turned my back on the dusty outside. I could smell supper on the stove, and warm sounds came from the kitchen, laughter and the sound of my siblings lightly quarreling. My heart swelled to bursting.

I may have been leaving behind part of my past, but I could take with me all that was important. As I sat down at the table, everybody's voices swallowed me into their volume, and I was encased in the chaos of my family.

"Hey! Alex!" Barked Willie. "We been lookin' for ya."

Lily grinned at me, food mashed up in her mouth. "Alex, Bubba says he can run faster than you anyday," taunted my sister through her potato teeth. I huffed and turned to Willie.

"He did?! How dare he! I am your superior in every way, peasant," I tried to keep a straight face. Willie raised an eyebrow, and then raised his nose.

"Alex, you ain't got nothin' on this speedy little guy," he bragged, guffawing. My severe face crumbled and I joined my two best friends, laughing, letting the lightness of their company soothe my previously aching heart.

"You ain't little," I corrected him, poking Willie in the stomach. "You gettin' pretty chubby, Willie!" He made a horrified face, opening his mouth wide and looking from his stomach to me and back again.

Lily burst out cackling and threw a forkful of peas at Willie. He ducked. Willie and I exchanged glances, agreeing silently to make an alliance, and were just about to retaliate when Papa strode over from the stove and smacked us both across the back of our heads.
"No food fights," he warned. "We gonna leave this kitchen afore too long, and we'll leave it clean-like. Like civilized folk."

Willie and I protested the unfairness, turning to Papa, both pointing at Lily. "She started it!"

Lily made her eyes huge and shook her head. "No, Papa, no," she said, looking devilishly innocent.

Papa patted Lily on the head. "I know darlin', I know. It were y'mean lyin' siblings."

"Whaaaat?!" Willie and I chorused.

Papa laughed. "Don't get your knickers up'n twisted," he clucked. "I were only jokin'... Kinda."

I rolled my eyes and Willie threw a single pea at Papa. It hit him on the nose. He roared and plucked Willie straight outta his chair, and then he lumbered across to the front room and dumped Willie on the couch. Papa grabbed the cushions and covered Willie with them. He tucked them around Willie good, then walked back into the kitchen as if nothing had happened.

"Papa, what..." I said as he sat down.

Papa looked regally down his nose at me. "'Tis th' price to pay for tossin' y'peas," he declared.

Lily and I looked at each other, and then everyone broke out laughing. We heard Willie's muffled yelling from the other room.

"Ain't funny!"

CHAPTER TWENTY-NINE

The days dragged by with frightening speed. It was like a beautiful pain. This longing to leave, this longing to stay. But in the end, my wishes to escape this place far outweighed my reluctance. I stood before our empty front room, staring at the place where our old sofa used to be. It was early Sunday morning, our last Sunday. All the furniture was gone, either sold, given away or loaded onto the truck. Willie had been sleeping on the floor in Papa's room since we moved out the sofa.

All that remained in the house were our beds and the kitchen table. We had three meals left to eat on it. One day. I wandered back into the kitchen and leaned on the countertops, sighing. There were few things I would miss about this place, but one of them was definitely Sunday mornings. Our little church was a big part of my life, and it often gave me strength when none was to be found. I was going to miss Pastor Ross's sermons most of all. They always seemed to come at the right times.

I looked at the early morning light streaming through the window and sighed. I heard a yawn behind me and turned to see Lily trotting into the kitchen, rubbing her eyes. I nodded at her.

"Mornin', Alex," she drawled sleepily. I pulled on her ponytail; she swatted my hand away. I turned to see Papa opening the door. He stamped his boots and came inside.

"Willie with you, Papa?" I asked, wondering where he'd got to.

Papa shook his head. "No, I haven't seen him. He ain't up yet?" I shook my head. Papa laughed. "Ah well, lazy boy. I'll wake him. Gotta git to church soon." Papa turned and vanished down the hall. I turned back to the counter and grabbed some of the last food in our home. We had to eat a plain breakfast today. Bread and cheese. That was it. It was gonna be simple like that for a while. I was perfectly okay with it; we were leaving at last. Excitement and anxiety squirmed in my belly, making the prospect of eating hard to stomach anyway. I ripped a chunk of bread off the loaf and broke off some cheese, sitting down at the table. I was lost in thought.

Where would we go? Papa had said west, away from the dust and dying land. I was terrified but so, so excited. Everything was changing in our lives now, hopefully for the better.

"Alex, we gotta eat that, y'know," Papa pointed out. I started. I hadn't even noticed him come in. Looking down at my hand, I realized I was clenching my fist tightly, with the cheese hunk still inside it. Oops.

"Where's Bubba?" Asked Lily. Papa tore off some bread, scattering golden crumbs everywhere.

"He's comin'," Papa answered. "That boy is bone-tired." At that moment, Willie walked in. His face was turned down, real white and exhausted-looking.

"What's up with you, Bubba?" I queried.

Willie looked up slowly, his eyes circled by darkness. "I'm just so darn sleepy is all," he drawled, yawning. He looked down at the floor then, and I saw his eyes watering. I didn't know if it was from yawning, or...

Suddenly a thought struck me. Maybe Willie was real worried about leaving. That had to be it. He wasn't sleeping well cause he was scared, not to mention the floors in this house weren't so comfy. I felt sympathy flow through me. He looked awful. I smiled at my adopted brother.

"You'll feel better after church," I promised, "I always do." Willie looked at me slowly, his eyes tired and sad. He smiled and nodded, then sat down with us. We ate breakfast silently then, for some reason. Happiness wasn't far off, but we were all quietly thinking about our future and what it held for us. I was so afraid and so ready to face the unknown.

Willie made a face at the cheese on the table suddenly. "Somebody done squished up th' cheese?" He grumbled, reaching for it.

"Hey, if y'don't want it, give it to me," Papa said, patting his stomach. "I'm witherin' away."

Lily giggled and shook her head. "Papa, you get much bigger an' we gotta leave you behind," she snickered. I tried not to laugh.

"Yeah, that ole truck can't take y'weight," Willie said, gesturing at Papa's gut. Papa made an indignant face and turned his back on us pointedly, leaving the cheese abandoned on the table.

"Fine then, ye wretches. Have the food all to y'selves, and I hope you ain't enjoyin' it at all." All three of us fell on the food without a second thought. By the time Papa turned around, the cheese was crumbles on the table and we were choking with laughter through stuffed cheeks. There was soft cheese under my fingernails and bread crumbs on the table.

Papa looked upset. "S'cuse me for thinkin' my children cared 'bout my wellbein'," he pouted. There was only us laughing and choking for air in return.

It took the lot of us about thirty minutes to get ready and another twenty to walk to the church. By the time we got there, the sermon was about to start. All four of us filed in silently and sat down in a pew, looking expectantly up at Pastor Ross. He was a middle-aged man, rather on the short side, with slowly graying hair and a warm smile. Today his eyes sparkled with joy as he took the stand and began to speak. I wondered what today was about.

"Good morning, congregation," called the Pastor.

Several cries of "Good morning!" And "Hello, Pastor!" greeted him.

He nodded in acknowledgment and then began to speak. "Today I have something rather wonderful to speak of," said the Pastor, light glittering in his eyes. "Today, I intend to speak of the beyond." The congregation waited silently, interested. Heaven was a subject which nobody could ever know enough about.

"Now, all of us will pass away someday." Said the Pastor. "Someday, but hopefully not anytime soon," he joked with a bright smile, and everyone laughed. "When that happens, we'd all like to know where exactly our souls are headed," stated Pastor Ross. "That place is Heaven." He said firmly. He gestured into the congregation. "All of you have lost loved ones," he exclaimed, gesturing widely, "and who wouldn't like to see them again!" The congregation clapped and whistled.

I glanced at Willie. His eyes were still drawn and sad, but some hope was lit in their depths. I wondered if he was thinking of his parents. I knew where my mama was, and that had always comforted me.

Pastor Ross strode to the edge of his platform and waved his hands in the air, stomping a foot to accent his words. He was an excitable fellow. "Folks, what kind of God would our God be, if he didn't have a place prepared for us after death!" He cried. His eyes travelled the pews. He waved his hands for attention. "I have a question. Who here would create something absolutely intricate and beautiful, a golden painting, a cherished photograph, a sculpture worked hard on; and then just throw it away after a few years?"

People shouted out, 'No!" and "Not me!"

"*Who here,*" exclaimed Pastor Ross, "would turn their back on their own child?"

Suddenly the back of my neck prickled. I turned and saw Grandfather sitting in the very last pew, head down and shoulders hunched. The person sitting next to him took my breath away.

Mrs. Johansson. Grandmother was in church.

I had never seen either of them here before, but there they were, clear as day. Grandpa looked to be crying. *Who would turn their back on their own child?* Pastor Ross's words echoed in my mind. Mrs. Johansson's arms were crossed, her head turned defiantly to the side, but I thought I could see her trembling. God was working here. I turned back to the front of the church.

"As much as we, here, love our children and families, so much more, then, does God love His children!" Pastor Ross cried. "So much more then, does God want His children with Him for all eternity!" I glanced again at Willie. His eyelids were flickering. Was he trying not to cry in church? It was okay to cry in church. I hoped he knew that.

"We are the children, the royalty, the *disciples* of Jesus the Christ." Said Pastor Ross, beginning to wind down. I felt my blood stir and the corners of my mouth twitch into a smile as Pastor said we were royalty of Christ. I looked at Willie, but he seemed not to have heard. Disappointed, I turned back.

"Folks, listen," said Pastor softly. "My point is this. There are many who do not believe there is a Heaven, nor a Hell. But I tell you truly today, both of these places exist and are very real indeed. So we must be careful, we must fight for the souls of our neighbors and friends. No enemy is too great to be saved, no soul too lost to be found." I took in a sharp breath and turned to look behind me. Mrs. Johansson's face was stoic, but tears streamed down her face. Her husband took her hand and she broke, hiding away in the cloth of his shirt, weeping for all she had lost.

I felt light enter my soul and warm me from my core. My Grandmother was going to be okay. I would see her again someday, in a place far better than this broken world. Pastor Ross was finishing up his sermon.

"Today I hope I've given you all some inspiration. There are souls abounding in this world, all in need of a Savior. Go forth and be a light to them, and bring home the lost sheep of this world." He bowed his head, speaking a few final words. "Many of you have lost loved ones. You all should know that death is no match for the one great Savior." The congregation exploded into cheers, leaping up and applauding. We all broke into singing, with Pastor leading us.

I was smiling happily, stepping from side to side as we worshipped, when I noticed Willie was still sitting down. His face was paler than before, if that was possible. Tears were gathering in his eyes, and he sneezed. He saw me looking at him and quickly stood up, holding onto the pew in front of him for support. I narrowed my eyes in curiosity and worry, but turned away to let him have peace.

The song ended soon and Pastor dismissed us. Everyone broke into small knots of people, talking, laughing, and exchanging news. Papa wandered over to some of his friends, shaking hands and clapping backs. They knew we were leaving, so he was saying final goodbyes. I watched Lily run over to some small girls and hug them one by one. Turning, I saw Willie talking to an older woman. I smiled involuntarily.

Miss Sally Obadiah. Our old teacher. Willie must have been saying goodbye. He stood on tiptoe to hug the elderly woman goodbye, and then he waved me over. I said goodbye in turn, and realized I would miss seeing Miss Sally every once in a while. She was such a kind lady, more like a grandmother to me than I had ever had.

"You be careful, now," she warned, wiping tears away. "I won't be around to watch out for you kids." Emotion flooded behind my eyes and heart, and I hugged her.

"It's alright, Miss Sally," I assured her. "I've got Willie to watch me." I smiled at him, and he echoed my smile weakly. Papa called us over then, and we said goodbye to Miss Sally one last time. Then we walked away, and suddenly we were joining hands with each other and Lily, and walking out the door behind Papa, leaving, leaving forever, saying goodbye to the Church we'd known all our lives.

And then we were on our way home for the last time, to sit and prepare and finish packing up and really say goodbye. This was it. We were walking out of town now, headed toward our farm.

"Willie, are you sad about leaving?" I asked him, wanting to know what was on his mind.

He glanced at me as we scrambled up over a hill. "No, not particularly," he mused. He didn't sound sad. I was impressed by the big word he used.

"What?" I asked, thinking I had heard him wrong. He looked at me curiously, and I noticed how hard he was breathing as we walked.

"I'm happy as anyone here t'leave this place, mayhaps happier." He attested between breaths. Confusion swam in my head.

"I thought you were upset about all this," I said, puzzled.

Willie raised an eyebrow, rubbing at his chest with one hand. "No, ain't at all, really. Can't wait to get outta this dust hole," he said.

"Oh." I said, digesting his words. "Willie?"

"Yeah, Alex?"

I pushed my hair outta my face. "If you ain't afraid or sad, why you been so down-lookin' and tired?"

Willie shrugged. "I just ain't been feelin' too good, s'all. Sleepin' on yonder floor, prob'ly." And he smiled, sayin', "It don't matter none though, 'cause we're leavin' on the morrow. Bright and early."

He rubbed his eyes and took a deep breath. It sounded raspy. "Ain't never gonna have to help you in the fields no more, or sit about thinkin' what I coulda done to save my Pa," He said. My eyes burned. "No more people lookin' at me like... they pityin' me... the little orphan... boy..." And that was when Willie collapsed. He crumpled to the dirty ground in a heap before me, eyes shut, head hitting the ground.

And I screamed.

CHAPTER THIRTY

Thank God we weren't far from Doc Jones's office. Papa took one look at Willie lying on the ground, scarcely breathing, and he silently bent to pick him up in strong arms. Then as one, all three of us turned back toward the town. I took Lily's hand. I could feel her shaking. She was craning to look at Willie.

"Alex, is Bubba gonna be okay?" She said, sounding very small.

I tightened my grip on her hand. "Of course he is, Lily. He... he has to be." Papa was silent before us. I wanted to ask him, wanted to scream and cry and beg him to promise that Willie was going to be fine. But we didn't even know what was wrong. So with iron resolve, I held back my panic, doing my best to be strong for Lily. I looked at Papa and he nodded, so without a single word, I turned and ran back to the church. My heart pumped louder as I burst in and looked wildly about. People looked up at me in alarm. I wasn't paying them any mind. Where was the doctor? Finally I spotted him, conversing with some other men in a corner of the church. I dashed over and grabbed his arm.

"Doctor, sir, please... You have to come... It's Willie. Papa took him to your office." Doctor Jones looked down at me, blinked, and quickly bid farewell to the men. Then he hurried along with me, and we were on our way.

Time went racingly slow, and then we were crowded around our fallen brother. Willie lay on a thin cotton mattress, raised up on a wooden frame. It was a tiny room, with a tin sink and a cupboard of who knows what. The thin bed and two chairs were the only furniture. Papa turned to look at me.

"We can't wake 'im," he said shakily. "He won't... open 'is eyes." Minutes ticked by, and Willie's breathing was shallow. Thoughts pulsed in my head as I gazed at Willie. He was asleep. The kind of sleep that scares you.

The doctor's face was apologetic. *Why do you already look sorry?* I thought.

"Let's see what the problem is," he said. But his voice was formal, like he was going through the motions. A terrible feeling that he knew exactly what the problem was wormed into my mind. He placed a bag on the counter full of bandage wrappings and scissors and pill bottles and an old thermometer. He turned silently and took in Willie's unconscious form. I watched his face closely as some flicker of regret lit in his eyes, like a dying ember. Then it went out. He rubbed his face and turned to us.

"Tell me what happened." He ordered. I immediately looked to Papa.

"We was walkin' back from service, sir, an' Willie just fell." Papa explained slowly.

"He was coughing before, and rubbing his chest, too," I added, the details appearing in my mind bright and sharp. The doctor looked at me solemnly, then down at our brother, shaking his head ever so slightly.

"He always said he was feeling fine," the doctor muttered. I narrowed my eyes, heart beginning to thump. An image flashed into my mind of Willie knocking on his chest with one fist as he spoke to the doctor, standing in our front room after Lily was healed. *He always said he was feeling fine.* Doctor Jones's cheekbones were high, accentuating his drawn face as he turned to us.

"When his mother died I watched him closely for some time to ensure his well-being, and that's when I first noticed the symptoms," The doctor said. I struggled to listen, but all I could hear was a pounding in my ears, a flush of blood so loud and hot that I could scarcely sit still. I tried to tell my heart to relax but it ignored me. The doctor took a breath. Normally very direct, he seemed hesitant for once.

"When Willie was very young, I told his father what I knew of his ailment. I didn't expect him to even live this long, quite truthfully. It's very rare. But every time I talked to Willie, he claimed he was fine, said he was 'fitter'n an ox.'"

"Ailment?" Papa demanded. "What're y'sayin'? I don't understand!" He exclaimed, frustration cracking his voice. The doctor held up his hands, and suddenly everything was very quiet.

"Frank, I thought you knew about this, having adopted him and whatnot," said Doctor Jones quizzically, puzzled. I couldn't hear the doctor. Couldn't breathe. Even the use of Papa's name felt odd to my ears, adding to the foreign nature of this entire situation. This was wrong. This was all wrong.

"Yessir, he's my son now, but I ain't heard nothin' 'bout no fancy ailment. Please, tell me what y'speak of. Why won't 'e wake up?" Papa looked cold. The doctor bowed his head, looking once again at Willie's still form.

"When Willie was born, he had a hard time breathing. As he grew older, my suspicions were only confirmed."

I turned desperately to Willie, waiting for him to wake up, to throw something at me or call Lily 'Lil Monster' or tease Papa about his weight. I couldn't comprehend the doctor's words. But Willie's eyes were closed, his chest barely moving.

Dr. Jones still seemed to feel odd about the fact that we didn't know this already. I could hear it in his voice. "Most people have many years ahead of them, with good, strong hearts that don't wear down until all those years have passed." Papa kept grabbing his hair, and I saw the years come back to him. He had seemed so young with Lily's healing.

"Doctor," Papa pleaded. "What's that mean?

"The difference between regular people and this boy," continued the doctor, "is the state of his heart. From birth, his heart was only going to last so long. And it's a good bit shorter than your heart will last." I stared at the doctor. He made it sound like Willie's heart was a worn out bit of machinery.

"What's all this mean for 'im, Doc?" Papa asked, and a definite tone of panic had entered his voice.

The doctor straightened his glasses. "Frank," sighed the man apologetically, "Willie hasn't got long."

That was when I shut down and stopped feeling, stopped feeling anything at all. The doctor kept talking and I heard him but I didn't feel the words enter my mind.

"How long? A year? A month?" Papa breathed, his voice shaking, face drained of color.

"I would say less than a day, actually."

A wave of nausea crashed over me, my stomach threatening to overturn its contents all over the floor. *Breathe, breathe, breathe,* I thought. *This can't be real. He's fine. Willie's not going anywhere. He can't leave us now. Everyone's supposed to be safe.*

"I'm gonna die tonight?" We all turned as one to Willie, whose honey eyes were open. His voice was soft and tired, and in that moment I realized just how tired he sounded.

Too tired to go on much longer.

CHAPTER THIRTY-ONE

The next moments were a blur. Papa led Lily and me out of the room, and we sat out front on the bench. I ran my fingers over patterns in the old wood, feeling cold and dead inside. Papa talked quietly with the doctor down the hall. They'd left Willie in his room, alone. I wanted to run back in there, to talk to him and make him laugh... because as long as he was talking to me, he couldn't leave.

I took a deep breath. I felt sleepy, tired, like my body had run out of fuel. I understood now, finally. All the times Willie had grabbed at his heart, all the times he'd bent over, shutting his eyes, shielding his chest; every single one of them jabbed my mind like sharp knives.

Why didn't you notice? The thought swirled around in my head, painful, bright and accusatory.

I watched the world spinning on around us. From the bench outside the doctor's office, I could see trees and paths and bushes and flowers. Storefronts boasted their signs in big letters that were meaningless to me. Even on a Sunday, when the shops were closed up tight, the world was alive. A car trundled by on a meandering road, children sticking their thin arms out the windows and calling out in their joy to be alive. Birds flew past on their buoyant winds, singing of freedoms that Willie would never feel again. I watched a chipmunk skitter around the trunk of a tree and wished bitterly that I'd let Lily keep that stupid squirrel she'd found. Finally Papa walked outside to us. I looked up at him, Lily leaning on my arm. I noticed for the first time how hard our bench was.

"He says we can take 'im on home now," said Papa hollowly, Willie a crumpled bundle in his arms. I stood stiffly and pulled Lily up with me. She sniffled.

"Is he still awake?" I said softly. In response, Willie snorted.

"I can hear ya," he said, ever the spirited one, but he sounded weak and exhausted.

I put on a brave face for my brother. "Of course you can," I scoffed. "I... Of course you can." I trailed off limply.

Willie just sighed deeply and closed his eyes. And then we were walking home, the dusty landscape stretching out before us. Papa had shifted, carrying Willie piggy-back style. We walked in front of him.

"Joke's on you all," said Willie. "I ain't sick. Jus' wanted Pa to git some exercise."

Papa laughed. "Yer a right ol' tricker, Willard," he said. I felt almost angry to hear him laugh, but my surprise turned to understanding when I turned and saw the depths of sorrow in his eyes. Papa was being brave for Willie too. Lily had been silent since the doctor's office, and I looked down at her, wondering how she could possibly be feeling. She glanced at me and I tried to smile. Lily didn't say anything.

Finally, we were home. Papa walked carefully inside and to his bed, where he laid Willie down like a broken toy. The boy stirred and then fell asleep easily. He was so exhausted now, so fatigued and ready to sleep. Fear stirred inside me. *Sleep.* That's all that was going to happen. I didn't need to be upset. Willie was just gonna go to sleep, and never wake up...

Miserable, I sat down next to the bed. Leaning against the wall, I watched Papa and Lily walk out. Lily was rubbing her eyes. I couldn't leave Willie, though. I was gonna stay and wait for him to wake up. My eyelids slipped shut. Hours later, someone poked me in the stomach. I opened my eyes and gasped. Willie crouched before me, laughing, cheerful honey eyes new and healthy again. I stared at him in awe.

"Willie, you're safe!" I cried.

He smiled. "I'll always be safe..."

Then the dream faded and I woke up. Despair settled over me like a dark cloud as I took in Willie's huddled form, still sleeping, still sick. Still a broken toy with a worn-out part.

I stood up, stretching. Glancing outside, I realized it was nearing sundown. I must've dozed off for a while.

I stood over Willie, taking in his face. Trying to engrave it in my memory, for all the days to come that I'd have to live without him. *Don't.* I thought, closing my eyes tight. Hot tears welled behind them. I put a hand to my face, trying to stifle my sobs. This little boy had become my best friend, and my brother, and my partner in crime, and he'd saved my life, and I'd saved his. We were supposed to have each other's backs, forever. Anger pulsed through me, as fiery as the sun, but sooner than I thought possible, sorrow became my blood. Tears streamed down my face.

"Hey, you cryin' again?" came a voice. "Don't cry."

I opened my eyes. "Willie!" I exclaimed. "You're awake." He rolled his eyes. "Got tired o'sleepin'. Time to help you lot finish packin' up." He tried to get up, but I shook my head. He fell back down.

"Guess I didn't sleep long enough," he said gruffly. "I'm still tired." With that, he became a little boy again, the little boy I met in the church that long ago day. The one who asked, *Why not?*

"Willie," I said, feeling sick inside.

"Alex," he replied gently. "It's all goin' be okay."

I began to cry. Messily, and brokenly, with heaving sobs that felt like sand in my chest. "It's not okay," I said, feeling like someone was trying to take away my right arm.

"Yes, it is," Willie insisted. At that moment, Lily and Papa came in and stood near the bed. Fire burned in Willie's eyes, an energy that I hadn't seen there in a while.

"Lissen t'me, all of you," Willie rasped. "I ain't goin' last much longer. Lil Monster, don't," he said, as Lily began crying too.

But Lily ignored him. She pounded the bed frame, shouting. "It's not fair! God took Mama, and now you!" She wailed. "It's not fair! Why! WHY!" Lily screamed. Then she collapsed in sobs next to the bed, trembling.

Willie's voice shook. "C'mon, Lil Monster. Don't do this to me. Y'know God wants t'lemme stay." She looked up at him with desperate eyes and a voice full of hope. Everything inside me shattered into painful pieces of glass, ones that stabbed me everywhere.

"Then why don't He?" She demanded.

"Because." Willie blinked slowly, and a very odd smile grew on his face. "I never got to meet my ma," he said, "or yours, for that matter. And she's a pretty amazin' woman, from what I hear," he added, glancing at me. My tears had stopped. They wouldn't fall anymore.

"I wanna meet them. And see Pa again," he murmured. Lily looked down and wiped away her tears, sniffling and nodding. "You guys are goin' on your journey, and I'm goin' on mine." Willie declared softly.

"Willie, wait," I pleaded. "We haven't done it all yet. You said you could run faster than me!" I didn't want him to give in now. *Don't give up yet,* I wanted to say. Moments with Willie were flashing in my head now; every promise, every laugh, and every broken moment. The day I found out his parents were dead, and the bullies had thrown rocks at him. The day Willie took my petname for Lily and adapted his own. The oddest part was, though, I couldn't recall the exact moment that he became my brother.

"You said you could run faster than me," I said again, quietly.

"We'll have to wait a bit longer to find that out, Alex," Willie breathed out, a promise in his gaze. I nodded at him, the soulsickness returning to me. I understood the lost man that lived in Papa's eyes now.

Then my brother Willie closed his eyes for the last time.

CHAPTER THIRTY-TWO

Willie went to sleep that night, and part of me fell away with him, lost forever.

The night seemed darker without him, the days longer and hotter and meaner. The whole world seemed like it was missing something essential, and it was going to ache like that for a long time. But we were still leaving this place and all the darkness. And, well, if there was one thing Willie would want, it would be for us to laugh and be happy again. And so, the night he died, I promised to never give up laughter. I swore to honor him with humor for the rest of my days, and to never give up hope.

Most of all, I promised to never stop trusting God. It would be hard sometimes, I would be sad or angry or doubt would creep back in. But then I would remember Willie, and I would remember just who my God was. It was because of Him that I'd see Willie and Mama again someday. My life was going to be so utterly different without my bright-hearted brother by my side. I'd gotten so used to him, so fond of his light and his presence. The loss of Willie was the freshest, and it stung.

I still woke up missing Mama, sometimes. I wanted her to be by my side. I wanted her to sing to me, and to protect me when the darkness came to scare me out of sleep.

I wanted her to sing to me...

Hush little darlin', don't you cry,
God's looking down on you all tonight.
Don't fret dear child, Willie's home now,
Mama loves you so and you've made her proud.

Somewhere far behind the little family was a tiny outcropping of trees. Dusty and forgotten, with an impassive creek that fed an insignificant pond in the midst of the swaying foliage. Birds sang in their quiet paradise, fluttering between branches as birds do. Amidst the gentle day, sunlight filtered through the trees' canopy and struck the ground, illuminating scattered nut shells and rotting acorn tops.

A little creature snuffled along the base of a tree, its fur healthy and thick. The adult squirrel suddenly stopped, tiny paws held still in terror as the sound of cracking branches reached it. It raised its head, listening, and the sunlight glanced across the scarred-over tear in its right ear. Then the beast flew up the trunk of a tree and was gone.

For the rest of my life, the sight of glass always made me remember the dust, for dust is akin to sand; and even sand, destructive and painful as it can be, when combined with fire, my bane and enemy, can be purged into the brightest glass, reflecting my hope, denying my past...

About the author

Kelsie is a student in Atlanta, Georgia where she lives with her family and four dogs. She spends much of her time with her local youth group and with the friends she's made through church, enjoying life and serving others. She loves God with all her heart, but her family and friends are a close second. Creating tales and characters has been Kelsie's passion since she was old enough to speak. She is delighted to be able to use her gift to fabricate beautiful, family-safe worlds where young adults and teens can lose themselves in another reality. She expects to release several other novels of various genres as well as works of poetry in the coming years.

Made in the USA
Lexington, KY
26 June 2017